Essential Articles 2016

Articles, opinions, arguments, personal accounts, opposing viewpoints

In print in this book & online as part of Complete Issues

Complete Issues
articles · statistics · contacts

Complete Issues
articles · statistics · contacts

www.completeissues.co.uk

Your log in details:

Username: _CC Student_

Password: _resources_

D0416659

Essential Articles 2016

For effective independent learning

Essential Articles 2016 is part of Complete Issues, a unique combination of resources in print and online.

Complete Issues

Complete Issues gives you the articles, statistics and contacts to understand the world we live in.

The unique format means that this information is available on the shelf and on the screen.

How does Complete Issues work?

Using www.completeissues.co.uk you can view individual pages on screen, download, print, use on whiteboards and edit to suit your needs. It makes Essential Articles even more flexible and useful.

Complete Issues has been redesigned this year to make it even more user-friendly and flexible.

All the articles are available to view online and download as PDFs and there are there are references and links to other parts of Complete Issues - the archive of articles, the statistics and the website and contact details of relevant organisations.

The articles in the Essential Articles series, the statistics in Fact File and online contacts work beautifully together on the Complete Issues website to produce a choice of relevant writing, figures and links.

When you search for a topic you instantly generate a list of relevant articles, figures and organisations with a thumbnail of the page and a short description.

The **advantages of Complete Issues** over just googling are:

- **varied & reliable sources**
- **moderated - so appropriate for student use**
- **properly referenced**
- **beautifully presented**
- **adaptable for classroom use**
- **cleared for copyright**
- **links that are checked for safety and relevance**

You can search and browse individual elements of Complete Issues or all the parts together, past and present editions.

You can research a topic secure in the knowledge that you will find reputable sources and considered opinions.

Our **Focus Guides** offer a selection from Complete Issues as a starting point or quick and easy access to information on the most searched topics.

In addition to the online service, you have this attractive printed version always available. Its bright, magazine-style format entices readers to browse and enjoy while learning about current issues and dilemmas, making even difficult issues approachable.

Because you have both the book and online access you can use Essential Articles in different ways with different groups and in different locations. It can be used simultaneously in the library, in the classroom and at home.

Your purchase of the book entitles you to use Complete Issues on one computer at a time. You can find your access codes on your covering letter or by contacting us. It is useful to record them on page 1 of this volume.

You can also buy an unlimited site licence to make the service and the material available to **all** students and staff at **all** times, even from home.

If you do not yet have the other resources in Complete Issues - the statistics and the contacts - you can sample the service and upgrade here:

www.completeissues.co.uk

Complete Issues

articles • statistics • contacts

Contents

Image © Peter Marshall / Demotix/Demotix/Press Association Images

❝ I've been given six months to live about five times in my life... It's difficult to predict when you are going to die ❞

Page 21

Contents

© Ronnie Hughes

66 If your child is allowed to have inappropriate access to any game or associated product we will contact the Police and Children's Social Care 99

Page 64

Image © Keston Ott-Dahl

> 66 We never had the big talk... let alone why she'd just taken me and not both of us... I missed my little brother so much that first night 99
>
> Page 80

Contents

Image © Simon-Ragoonanan, manvspink.com

> ❝ It's like having liquid terror injected into your veins... You have an overwhelming sensation that something is very wrong. ❞
>
> Page 124

© Gabrielle Jackson

Contents

© Thorston Wulff

> “ He was really happy that he met me, because he could see that history does not have to repeat itself ”
>
> Page 169

Contents

Image © Rena Schild / Shutterstock.com

66 One day he will be slain in cold blood by a policeman who is supposed to protect him and his community 99
page 184

66 I like seeing individuals return home with a reformed attitude to their life and an improved understanding of the worthlessness of many 'essential' material possessions 99
page 196

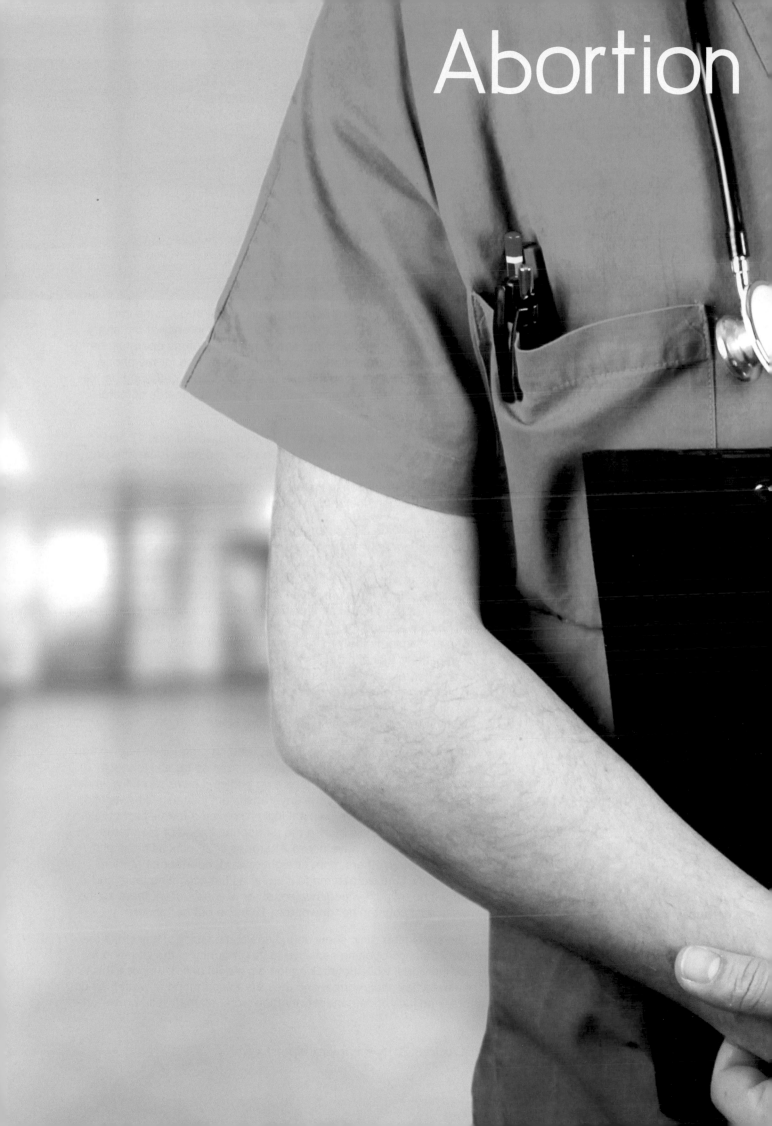

Abortion

Being an abortion doctor has taught me a lot about life

I've learned from the women I care for that it's never an easy decision and I'm grateful I can help them at a difficult time

Anonymous

SOME ISSUES:

Do you think it is important for abortion to be available on the NHS?

Why would there be "21 difficult decisions"?

Should people protest outside abortion clinics?

The writer wonders if she should "feel guilty". What makes the writer ask that question?

I slip out through the back door of the clinic, cut through the car park and cross to the far side of the road. I pick intently at the angry blisters emerging on the thumb and index finger of my operating hand, then shift my concentration to rummaging in my bag for my phone. Anything to avoid catching the eye of the protestors gathering on the opposite pavement, brandishing their gruesome placards of foetal parts.

I can't say this is exactly what I had in mind when I was 17 and writing my Ucas application, full of idealism and pride to be applying for such a noble profession. Probably not what my parents were thinking of either - it doesn't make for great dinner party conversation having an abortion doctor for a daughter.

But somehow here I am. I made a decision not to conscientiously object and I am now nearing the end of my abortion-care training. If I'm honest, I haven't found it emotionally easy (and I suspect neither have those closest to me!) but I'd never go back and change that decision. Not only have I received excellent tuition, but, perhaps more importantly, I have learnt much about life from the women I have cared for. They have taught me that pregnancy at the wrong time, with the wrong person, or in the wrong situation, can be a very lonely and unsympathetic place to be. One young woman confided in me that she'd rather take three buses home after her medical procedure and risk bleeding on the bus than have to ask a friend or family member for a lift, and therefore disclose her situation. I loaded her up with sanitary towels and silently hoped for the best.

I have performed 21 abortions today, ending pregnancies in women ageing from 16 to 44, who have travelled from as far as Northern Ireland to regain control over their own bodies. I have carefully sieved through aspirate to identify the tiny translucent jelly-fish-like gestation sac at five weeks. I have painstakingly removed a foetus part by part at 23 weeks and watched the ultrasound image of the uterus shrink back to size. I have heard 21 stories of 21 difficult decisions, some agonising, others more straightforward, but not one of them taken lightly. One woman made it as far as the operating table and changed her mind. I wiped away another woman's silent tears as the anaesthetist counted her down from 10 as he put her under.

The staff in the clinic show boundless compassion. They strike the perfect balance of being sensitive to the enormity of the situation for each individual while not making too big a deal of it. I suppose this is their everyday, their normal and they are experienced at what they do: there is no lack of demand for abortion work, as that well-known "one

Image © J. Bicking / Shutterstock.com

> I have heard 21 stories of 21 difficult decisions, some agonising, others more straightforward, but not one of them taken lightly.

in three women in the UK" statistic demonstrates. My training also serves to remind me that there is no one type of woman who experiences unwanted pregnancy.

I've seen as many professional women in their 40s as chaotic girls in their teens; and the majority have been using some form of contraception, albeit unsuccessfully. Many of the women are already mums. Some are devoutly religious. Some have been advised to have an abortion of a much-wanted pregnancy for medical reasons or severe foetal abnormalities. One woman I encountered had been trying to conceive for many years and finally got pregnant by IVF, only to be given this devastating recommendation.

It has not yet become my everyday and my normal. I wonder if it will ever feel like that. As I leave clinic, I actually feel slightly elated from the work - I have learnt skills far beyond my expectations and I feel gratified to have been involved in helping women out in a vulnerable

and sometimes desperate time. I glance back at the pro-life contingent and I wonder whether I feel guilty, or whether I should. There is a stir as a wide-eyed woman leaves the entrance of the clinic; she flinches when she sees the crowd and bows as if to hide her face. As I walk away I know these protestors have inadvertently answered my question. As long as unplanned pregnancy exists, we need to help women in this unfortunate situation, not harass them. Abortion can improve life and prevent harm; pro-choice, to me, does not mean anti-life.

I breathe my customary sigh of relief as I close my front door behind me and kick off my shoes. My boyfriend hears the latch and calls from the kitchen to ask me about my day. I mutter something nondescript, skimping on detail, then get straight to the point: "How about a glass of wine?".

The Guardian, 22 June 2015 © Guardian News & Media 2015

> As long as unplanned pregnancy exists, we need to help women in this unfortunate situation, not harass them.

More very premature babies are surviving.

Does that mean it is time to review the abortion law?

A normal pregnancy last for 40 weeks. The law in the UK allows termination of a pregnancy up to the 24th week. This was the earliest date at which a very premature baby was considered viable - able to survive separately from its mother.

However, as medicine advances, more babies who are born very early are surviving. Does that mean that the basis for the law has shifted and it should be revised?

YES

If the whole basis for the existing time limit is whether a child can survive, then it is time it was changed. There has been a dramatic rise in the number of babies born at 23 weeks who survive. In some hospitals, such as University College London, over 85% of babies born at 23 weeks survived. That alone is enough to make a change in the law worth considering - being born very prematurely is no longer a death sentence.

Look at three individual cases reported in newspapers about very pre-term babies who are thriving. Lucas Moore was born in Coventry at 22 weeks. He weighed less than half a kilo and had a bleed on the brain. Doctors feared that even if he survived he would be severely disabled. But Lucas fought for life and in August 2014 he celebrated his first birthday in good health. Lily Burrows was given only a 5% chance of survival when she was born at 23 weeks weighing barely half a kilo. But in Autumn 2014 she started primary school.

You can see for yourself how well a very premature baby can survive by visiting the Facebook page 'Little Daisy-Mae'. When she was born, at 25 weeks, her father started the page to keep friends and family informed of her progress. It now has more than 23,000 likes and her father's book 'Little Daisy-Mae: The Girl Who Couldn't Wait' helps to raise money for the care of premature babies.

These are not isolated cases. Medical studies of premature babies are being conducted which follow them throughout their lives. A study which started in 1995 has subjects who are now approaching their twenties.

Lucas, Lily, Daisy-Mae: all three are little miracles who prove that modern medicine requires us to look again at the 24 week abortion limit, because within that limit, children like Lucas, like Lily and like Daisy-Mae - children who could survive and thrive are being terminated.

SOME ISSUES:

Do you think improvements in premature survival rates affect the issue of abortion?

Is there ever a situation when abortion is not justified?

Do you agree that abortion should be free to all?

Should the law have any say in this or should it be left to the woman and the medical staff?

What do you think are the pros and cons to allowing legal abortion?

NO

It is something to be celebrated that loved and wanted children born to willing mothers are surviving at earlier terms and at higher rates. But the medical improvements do not justify imposing on unwilling mothers the burden of an unwanted child!

The survival chances for pre-term babies are not the same in every case. The best rates are achieved in specialist settings, with expert medical staff and properly equipped intensive care units. Survival rates for these very fragile and dependent infants were much less good in 'ordinary' medical settings.

The gestation period is crucial: those born alive at 27 weeks have an 87% chance of surviving, at 28 weeks it is 92% and at 29 weeks, 95%. But for babies born before 24 weeks, survival is still very much in doubt.

Surviving birth is not the end of the story. There is a very high financial and a still higher emotional cost to supporting these children throughout their lives. The welcome stories of children who have survived an early birth and have prospered are news precisely because they are rare.

While survival rates have improved, rates of disability in these pre-term babies have remained constant. The strategies that have promoted their survival have not changed their high risk of disability, even with specialist care. According to the EPICure study (which recorded all births in the UK between 20 weeks and 25 weeks, six days): 'the number of babies leaving neonatal units with abnormalities on their brain showing on ultrasound scans, and with lung, bowel and eye problems are very similar to what we found in 1995'. When the researchers tracked a group of these babies to the age of six, they found 22% had disabilities such as cerebral palsy and an inability to walk, low mental scores, blindness or profound hearing loss. 24% had moderate disability, leaving them with special needs.

In 2013 only 1% of abortions in England and Wales were conducted at 20 weeks or over. In contrast, 79% were conducted at less than nine weeks. Although the predominant reason for abortion remains the same (risk of injury to the physical or mental health of the woman) there is a notable increase, as the gestation weeks continue, in women choosing abortion because of a substantial risk of severe abnormality or handicap in the child. 389 women underwent abortion for this reason in very early pregnancy in 2013. This increased to 2,343 women in the later weeks (13 weeks onward), including 904 women who made this choice after the 20th week.

Newspapers may give us the impression that those choosing abortion are young and irresponsible. But Clare Murphy, a director at the British Pregnancy Advisory Service, has explains that "The women who have abortions are the same women who have children, who suffer miscarriages, who have IVF. We act like it's the sole preserve of the young and the reckless and feckless... but the majority of women we see in our clinics were using contraception at the time they became pregnant." In other words, we are generally discussing the choices of adult women who have made a conscious decision not to become pregnant. It's a decision about their own bodies and their own lives which should be respected and should be theirs alone.

Reducing the abortion limit would penalise the small percentage of women who need a late-term abortion, increase the number of children living with severe problems and is not justified by the improvements in survival rates.

Let medical practitioners concentrate their time and efforts on saving these accidental early births but it cannot be argued that they are really viable when so many pre-term birth results in lifelong dependency.

"The majority of women we see in our clinics were using contraception at the time they became pregnant."

Sources: Various

Image © Peter Marshall / Demotix/
Demotix/Press Association Images

Protests at abortion clinics - harassment or free speech?

A woman stands on the street arguing fiercely with a group of anti-abortion protesters. She questions a man about whether he is filming women entering a clinic. She rebukes the protestors passionately about making women feel guilty and about judging people without knowing their circumstances. She is just a passer-by, but the fact that she is obviously in the late stages of pregnancy herself seems to add force to her support for other women's right to choose differently. Against the wall there is a huge, graphic poster of an aborted foetus - a tiny, partly-formed arm, raised and blood-covered.

In another part of London, a middle aged woman with curly grey hair ask a young protestor "Why are you here outside my doctor's surgery?" She tells a TV news reporter that she fought for a woman's right to choose to end a pregnancy and does not want to see protests at her 'wonderful' GP surgery.

These are two examples from YouTube videos in which people question the right of anti-abortion protestors to demonstrate outside clinics and surgeries.

The British Pregnancy Advisory Service has experienced an increase in the number of anti-abortion protests outside abortion clinics, with some activists standing directly outside and blocking entrances, hindering access to advice, counselling and medical treatment.

SOME ISSUES:

Do you agree that abortion should be legal?

Do you agree with the idea of free speech?

Who do you sympathise with? Can you see the opposite point of view?

Are there ever inappropriate places to protest?

How would you deal with this situation?

As protests have become more frequent, there have been calls for 'buffer zones' around clinics which would keep the protestors at a distance. The hope is that this would prevent the area around medical centres becoming 'a battle zone' of protest and counter-protest in which staff as well as patients are intimidated.

Such zones have been tried in other countries. In Canada, for instance, the state of British Columbia has buffer zones of different sizes around doctors' surgeries, hospitals, clinics and medical workers' homes. Other states have limited the numbers who can protest or pray outside clinics. Toronto has instituted a 3 metre 'floating' buffer zone meaning protestors cannot come close to patients and staff.

People who object to the protests suggest that they make already vulnerable women feel uncomfortable and that they attempt to make women feel wrong or guilty. They say the cameras used by the protestors particularly worry the women, who fear being filmed and then publicly 'shamed'. At an already very emotional time, the protest feels intrusive and threatening to them. They argue that women who attend an abortion clinic have not taken the decision lightly and should not have a difficult choice challenged in a way that is psychologically and sometimes physically intimidating.

One woman told Channel 4 news how she felt harassed on her way into a clinic by the sight of plastic foetuses and graphic pictures of the process. "They weren't aggressive or loud, but it was emotional blackmail," she said.

Carlos Javier Sanchez/AP/Press Association Images

Women have not taken the decision lightly and should not have a difficult choice challenged in a way that is psychologically and sometimes physically intimidating

The protestors, on the other hand, generally feel that their cause outweighs any discomfort that they impose on the women or the general public.

In the cases on YouTube the protestors were from a group called Abort67 whose aim, according to their website, is "to make abortion unthinkable and to see the law give full protection to the unborn. The most effective way to change public policy is to first change public opinion."

Abort67 is part of a wider group CBRUK. Its parent group - The Center for Bio-Ethical Reform - was formed in the United States in 1990. Protests and even violence against abortion providers are much more prevalent in the US and the debate there is much fiercer.

This group sees a foetus, from conception, as a viable human being, they feel they are justified in acting to prevent abortion

This group sees a foetus, from conception, as a viable human being, they feel they are justified in acting to prevent abortion. To those who put the hardest cases to them - such as "What about rape or incest?" - their answer is "Why should the unborn child be punished because of his/her father's crime?" They see the rights of the foetus as the highest priority and therefore have little time for the counter-argument of a woman's right to choose. Instead they argue that they have the right to put their point of view and that a buffer zone would interfere with that.

The organisation 40 Days for Life holds prayer vigils outside abortion clinics. They deny that these cause harassment and distress. A spokesman said: "We've been organising prayer vigils since 2010 - legal and peaceful vigils - We've seen hundreds of women in London choose life because of pavement counselling, and this has helped people in need." His group, and other anti-abortion groups, dislike the use

of graphic images by Abort67 but strongly defend their "legal right to public protest". They see the demand for buffer zones as restricting the right to free speech. For example, the campaign group Right to Life says, "Regardless of what we think of the prudence or wisdom of individual protests or protestors, all people of good will should zealously, guard our freedoms to act and speak in the public square."

Abort67 has the slogan Push Back, echoing its desire to turn back all pro-abortion laws. "We want to see a generation that is bold and fearless to stand up under the pressure to go with the flow."

The British Pregnancy Advisory Service, within a coalition of 19 organisations, including the Royal College of Midwives, Marie Stopes International and the End Violence Against Women Coalition, has launched the Back Off campaign, saying: "We believe limiting the ability to interfere with women as they try to access a lawful medical service in confidence does not represent an undue restriction on our existing freedoms. These people have every right to campaign for greater restrictions on women's reproductive choices and there are plenty of opportunities and locations in which to do so. However the space immediately outside a clinic should not be one of them."

Abortion is a legal right in this country, and so is free speech. Does ensuring free and unhindered access to clinics deny people the right to peaceful protest? When two rights collide how do you decide which has the greater priority?

Sources: Various

Abortion is a legal right in this country, and so is free speech! When two rights collide, how do you decide the greater priority?

Assisted dying

Mercy or murder?

Should we change the law on assisted suicide?

Attempting to kill yourself is not a crime; but anyone who assists another person to end their life risks up to 14 years in prison. Campaigners want to change the law, so that terminally ill adults could request life-ending medication from a doctor. However there are equally strong challenges to this campaign from those who believe a change would place vulnerable people at risk.

THE CURRENT LAW:
NO, DON'T CHANGE THE LAW

The law is clear and simple: we do not kill other people. You cannot deliberately end another person's life - that's murder. When people become suicidal we try to help and support them. If someone was threatening to end their life we would try to persuade them not to do it - this is a fundamental instinct. Our law reflects this basic teaching of Christianity and other religions.

The law may seem to be harsh but because of the way it works, each case can be looked at separately and treated seriously. In most cases people who help their loved ones to end their lives are not prosecuted, or if they do go to court their circumstances are taken into account. Causing the death of someone else should never become routine.

YES, DO CHANGE THE LAW

At the moment, UK law sees no difference between someone who acts in a malicious way to take a life and someone who helps another adult who has made an absolutely clear decision that they want to end their life.

People who have thought about this, and have concluded that their life is no longer worth living, need to be able to die with dignity and without worrying about their loved ones or their doctors being charged with a crime simply for carrying out an act of mercy.

The law needs to reflect the fact that someone who has made a definite, well-informed and final decision to end their life might not be in a position to do so without help. People who are able-bodied can freely choose to end their lives. Isn't it the ultimate discrimination to deny this right to someone just because they need assistance?

SOME ISSUES:

Considering all these reasons for and against assisted suicide, do you think the law should be changed?

Who ultimately has the right to decide whether a person should live or die?

What do you think are the pros and cons of legalising assisted suicide in this country?

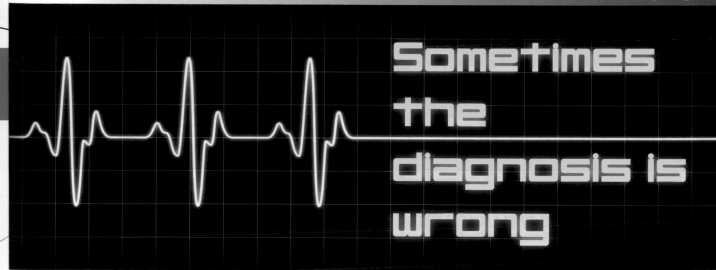

Sometimes the diagnosis is wrong

END OF LIFE CARE:
NO, DON'T CHANGE THE LAW

Care at the end of life should be and can be genuine care. In our society we should have the attitude that we will care for those who are suffering, not that we will simply make an end of it. We must not make people feel that the only end to their suffering is to shorten their life, and we should not have a law that implies that. Good end of life care should mean a gentle, pain free and natural conclusion to life. In general doctors do not wish to be involved in terminating a life.

YES, DO CHANGE THE LAW

We know that not everyone is lucky enough to receive the highest standard of end of life care. The majority of people die in hospital and doctors already make decisions about whether it is 'worth' resuscitating, treating or even feeding some patients. They are 'allowed' to die. For someone who is terminally ill that decision should not be in the hands of a social worker, a doctor or, in the back of a patient's mind, the courts. It is their life, their choice and nobody else's.

When people refuse treatment - for example cancer patients who have had enough aggressive therapies - we respect their decision. The decision by terminally ill patients to take an active approach to ending their life with dignity should also respected.

EXPERIENCE IN OTHER COUNTRIES:
NO, DON'T CHANGE THE LAW

Oregon, in the USA, changed its laws 10 years ago. There are now four times as many assisted suicides as before. 40% of those requesting to end their life say they feel they are a burden on friends and family - nothing to do with their own pain.

In Holland there has been a rise in patients with mental illness using assisted suicide. Often the suffering that was making life 'unbearable' was really just being old, lonely or bereaved - conditions that can be helped. People should not be considering suicide for these reasons - and they probably would not consider it under the current UK law.

YES, DO CHANGE THE LAW

Although we can say that the number of assisted deaths in Oregon has gone up fourfold, that still means that last year fewer than 100 people made use of the law on assisted dying. The numbers themselves do not tell us about the amount of suffering in each individual case - and it is the individual cases and individual choices that we should be concerned with.

It is too soon to say whether changes in the law really lead to changes in attitudes. If attitudes to dying change, will that inevitably be a change for the worse?

Whose life is it?

Belgium legalised euthanasia in 2002 and has extended it beyond terminally ill adults. It can now be used in cases of intense pain and psychological distress, and for terminally ill children, with their parents' consent.

Frank Van Den Bleeken, a serial rapist and murderer who had served 30 years in prison, applied for euthanasia because his life sentence was causing him "unbearable psychological suffering". The request was considered and at first it seemed it would be granted.

The sisters of his last victim, Christiane Remacle, a 19-year-old girl raped and strangled to death by Van Den Bleeken, called for him to "languish in prison" rather than be allowed a swift release. "No doctor or expert ever came and asked how we were. And then we hear his lawyer on the radio saying how tough it was for him to be abandoned in prison."

The procedure was cancelled and Van Den Bleeken was to be transferred to a specialist treatment facility.

When is the right time?

Business man Jeffrey Spector was aged 54 when he travelled to Switzerland to the Dignitas clinic to end his life. A keep-fit enthusiast, he had a cancer in his spine which threatened to paralyse him from the neck down. He said, "I am going before my time but I am not scared. I believe what I am doing is in the best long-term interests of my family. They disagree with that of course but they accept I have my own opinion... I know I am going too early but I had consistent thoughts without peer pressure.

It had to be a settled decision by a sound mind. If I am paralysed and cannot speak what hope is there?"

When 'mercy' becomes murder

Heather Davidson was sentenced to life imprisonment, with a minimum term of nine years after she smothered her friend David Paterson (aged 81) at his care home. She had called Macmillan Cancer Support in tears about what she saw as his suffering and the indignity of his end. She told them she could not bear to see him go on like that and "If he was a dog he would have been put down months ago."

However, Mr Paterson had always expressed his opposition to euthanasia, saying: "It will be God's decision and only God's when it is time to meet my maker."

The family's lawyer said: "Her decision to end his life deprived Mr Paterson of what he and his family most wanted - a natural, private and dignified death. Her actions also denied his close family of being able to say their final farewells and to grieve privately."

Sources: Various

'I've been given six months to live probably about five times in my life...'

Body image

YOU CAN'T JUDGE A BOOK BY ITS COVER ...

BUT SHOULD APPEARANCE INFLUENCE DECISIONS IN A COURT OF LAW?

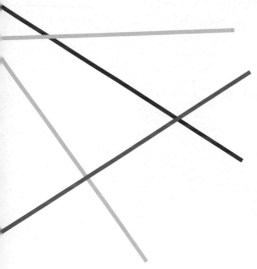

Early in 2015 Jason Barnum appeared in court in Anchorage, Alaska, accused of shooting a police officer. He pleaded guilty to attempted murder, burglary and felony (serious crime) in possession of a weapon. The court heard about his record of imprisonment, his 14 previous convictions and his heroin addiction. However, it seemed that not just his actions but also his appearance was on trial.

Barnum has had one side of his face tattooed to resemble a skull. A 'third eye' is drawn in the middle of his forehead. He has a crown of thorns encircling his bald head and another skull tattooed on the top of it. Along with numerous other tattoos he has one which earned him the nickname 'eyeball' - the white part of his right eye has been inked to give the appearance of a solid mass of deepest black.

In court, the Chief of Police in Anchorage argued that this appearance told us all about the mindset and attitude of the man. He said: "I think Jason Barnum decided a long time ago that his life was about being hostile to people. I'd like you to take a look at Mr Barnum."

Barnum agreed that his "beautiful face" had deprived him of work because it put off potential employers. He admitted "Everybody knows that I'm not the nicest guy. I understand that what I did was wrong. I can't take none of it back."

Undoubtedly Barnum's appearance is meant to be disturbing. The US tattoo artist who started the practice of eyeball tattooing intended to bring "realm of fantasy into everyday life" by injecting eyeballs with blue, green, red or black ink. But he advises people to stay away from darker colours, "I tell them you're going to look frightening forever to the majority of people you encounter. You might find people have trouble connecting with you or looking at you because they can't follow your iris."

SOME ISSUES:

Why do you think people modify their bodies?

Are some ways of modifying your body 'acceptable' and others which would make you an 'outsider'?

Why are we more comfortable with some forms of modification than others?

Should we judge someone based on how they choose to decorate their body?

Should a jury?

His nickname is 'eyeball' – the white part of his right eye has been inked to a solid mass of deepest black.

> **Barnum agreed that his "beautiful face" had deprived him of work because it put off potential employers**

In fact the colouring of the white of the eye is not classic tattooing - it isn't really possible to create a design - instead the ink is injected into the eyeball. The procedure comes with major risks of reaction to the ink, over-injection, sensitivity, headaches and, of course, the risk that you may regret it!

There is a whole subculture of drastic body modification which goes much further than the tattoos and piercings that we have become used to seeing over the last few years. 'Body modders' see their adaptations of the human form as self-expression and improvement, but to those outside the subculture it can seem like distortion. Amongst the most popular body modifications are pointed elf-like ears and split, snake-like tongues. Some people have had transplants of silicone under their skin to give the appearance of budding horns on their heads or of reptile-like spines. Hi-tech modifications in development include magnets implanted under the finger tips and lights under the skin which would flash to the beat of music.

At Barnum's trial, the Chief of Police in Anchorage acknowledged his right to change his appearance, a view that extreme body modders would agree with. Nevertheless, he asked the trial to draw conclusions about Barnum's character from his tattoos, "He has the right to do this to himself and to express himself. We can't sentence him for that, but I think we can consider a guy's attitude and his behaviour."

So was Barnum's sentence the product of a fair judgement about what he had done or did his appearance play a part in his being sentenced to 22 years in jail?

What can someone with horns or a split tongue expect if they come before a judge and jury? Extreme transformations are bound to create fear or repulsion or, at the very least, a sense of being outside society. Is it reasonable to ask ordinary people to set aside their own reactions to ensure a fair trial? Or is it more likely that, like the police chief suggested, they will 'take a look' and draw their own conclusions?

Sources: various

'Body modders' see their adaptations as self-expression and improvement

Photo posed by model

Body Image Issues Are Not Just For Women

Jessica Lovejoy

SOME ISSUES:

Why do you think magazines and clothing shops promote such a narrow range of body types?

How do these body types affect people's idea of body image?

What are the typical pressures put on men and women in terms of the 'ideal' body type?

Why is it important to encourage a positive body image?

What can we do to make sure people develop a positive body image?

Body image issues are prevalent within our perfection-focused society. We are told to conform to impossible beauty standards, to fit a certain body shape and that if we don't look a certain way, we aren't beautiful. We have diet fads and crazes thrust upon us to try and encourage us to get that "perfect" figure that everybody seems to want and we are picked apart by the media and told to rebuild ourselves in their perfect ideal. But women are not the only ones to suffer.

Men are also given the 'perfection' blueprint. They should be strong, muscular, show no emotion. They are told constantly to "Man Up" and to "Be a Man." The size of a man's penis is constantly

bought up in many a conversation between girlfriends over lunch, much like his performance in the bedroom.

Some of you ladies reading this may scoff and roll your eyes, thinking "Welcome to my life!" Yes, us women have had to deal with this sort of scrutiny for much of their lives, but we shouldn't be under the assumption that men don't know the feeling. Truth be told, we are all victims of the media. No one is safe.

Only within the last few years have fuller-figured women been in the media. We have our own plus-size models and clothing stores that cater from size 14 upward, and even chain stores carry plus-

Taut, toned, oiled and well-endowed men grace the glossy pages of almost every magazine you reach for... It is an unrealistic expectation for men.

size clothing. The fuller-figured gentleman does not have this luxury. You will almost never see a heavyset lumberjack-esque man gracing the cover of a clothing catalogue. Or a fashion magazine. Or an in-store poster.

You will, however, see taut, toned, oiled and well-endowed men gracing the glossy pages of almost every magazine you reach for, every chain clothing store and everywhere else. It is an unrealistic expectation for men. And a lot of women love the way these male models look, so that adds fuel to the fire in the male mind. Like women, they feel they have to fit this extreme standard in order to be found attractive by the opposite sex.

We, as females, have been dealt a cruel hand by way of the media. Our bodies truly are under scrutiny. They tell us that celebrities with curves are too fat, but when those same celebrities decide to lose weight, they are too thin and the media suggests that they are suffering from an eating disorder.

Now, we don't keep quiet anymore. We kick and scream and tell the media we want more diversity of size, sex and gender, and sometimes they listen. But men, like they've always been taught, remain silent. They don't complain and they go with it. The 'strong, silent type' is how men are conditioned.

When a chubby school boy is bullied by his peers about his weight, barely an eyelid is batted. When he is called a slob by his workmates, he is expected to let it roll right off his back. In today's society, the ideal man should be tall, rugged, handsome, muscular,

be well-endowed, be an excellent lover, be strong, emotionless.

A picture has been circulating of a young man holding up a handwritten sign reading "It's just as hard to be Ken as it is to be Barbie." I posted this particular picture on my personal blog to very mixed reviews. One particular blogger reblogged the picture and commented "Cry harder white boy."

This is not the way things like this should be handled. We should be understanding of those men who do suffer from body image issues and eating disorders, we shouldn't be scolding them because we've had to experience this cruelty for longer. As a whole, we all need to understand the damages the media can cause. If we can do that, we will be well on our way to a more body positive society for all.

Undue pressure is put on men by women, their friends, other men and their parents, especially their fathers. "Be a Man" is something that is easily said, but carries a lot of weight. Slamming a man with this phrase is telling him that he has to bury his emotions and his feelings, to take life on the chin and to never show weakness. If he cries, he is weak; if he is kind, he's a wimp. This simple phrase has the ability to be crippling. Telling the young man this will give

him extreme feelings of inadequacy. It insinuates that he's not man enough, he's not strong enough.

Nowadays, hitting the gym is in. Bulking and gaining is the next big thing. Being big and muscular is where it's at. Is it any wonder why the thin gentlemen and the chubby gentlemen avoid the gym? At least us women have ladies-only gyms that promote friendship and acceptance to all. Hitting the gym is a big deal for anyone who hasn't ever been, or doesn't go frequently, and that is made harder by the snickers and glares received from more muscular men over by the weights.

The truth is women are not the only ones who can suffer from poor self-image. And to assume that men don't is absurd.

As a society, we're all being force-fed images of this race of "perfect" people. We're told how to look good in certain outfits and how to dress for our shape; we're encouraged to lose the baby weight because Kim Kardashian did so in record time; and we're urged to get fit by Summer.

Whatever your gender, we are not safe from low self-esteem and poor body image caused by much of our society and our media.

Don't buy into it.

Huffington Post, 26 May 2014

"Be a Man" is something that is easily said, but carries a lot of weight.

Jessica Lovejoy is a Positive Body Image Advocate and writer.
Follow her page Positive Body Image Inspiration on Facebook: facebook.com/positivebodyimage89.
You can also follow her blogs:
positivebodyimageinspiration.tumblr.com
bodypositivityforthemodernman.tumblr.com
And read more of her articles at her Huffington Post Blog:
m.huffpost.com/us/author/jessica-lovejoy

laws like this, if they were ever actually enforced, are long overdue for the sake of models themselves. But to suggest that this will have any impact on the rates of eating disorders is tantamount to saying that eating disorders are essentially about silly women wanting to look like models, which is precisely the kind of condescension I long ago learned to expect from people when they talk about a mental illness that largely affects women and girls.

Looking at photos of skinny models makes a lot of girls and women feel bad about themselves...

That looking at photos of skinny models makes a lot of girls and women feel bad about themselves is not in doubt; and for that reason, again, these well-intended laws are perfectly welcome. But can we please make the overdue distinction between women suffering from body image issues and actual eating disorders, which are a specific mental illness?

Social issues do come into play with eating disorders: when, as a young woman, you realise how much value society places on your body, it makes sense to use that as the instrument with which to express your unhappiness. But believe me, it's not just fashion that sends women this message, and it's not even about thinness. It's about the way women are still valued

primarily by their physical appearance. Which brings me to my next point.

At the far more stupid end of the spectrum, a certain Dr Aric Sigman - whom readers of a certain vintage will remember as the agony uncle on the kids' TV show Live & Kicking - gave a speech at a teachers' conference in London this week, in which he suggested that the real key to fighting eating disorders among women is - can you guess? Can you? - men. "Men are an untapped army ... Knowing what men think can serve as an antidote to the prevailing assumptions that feed body dissatisfaction," Dr Sigman claimed, sounding thrillingly as though he was reading Alan Partridge's take on eating disorders.

...but can we please make the distinction between body image issues and actual eating disorders?

It turns out, Dr Sigman exclusively revealed, that men like female curves. This changes everything, ladies. "Men are an untapped army who need to become aggressively vocal," he concluded. Because if there's one thing women around the world have been lacking, it's men telling them exactly what they find attractive in a lady.

Dr Sigman - who is, amazingly, described as "a leading educational psychologist" - seems not to have considered the perfectly obvious possibility that one potential factor behind eating disorders in women, especially anorexia, is a fear of being sexualised, which is just one reason why it tends to take root during puberty. If men had told me when I was starting to get ill at the age of 13 that they really dug womanly hips, I would have begged to be locked up in a psychiatric ward for life out of sheer terror.

So why did I stop eating? Because I was unhappy. Because I didn't know how to express it vocally. Because I didn't understand I was allowed to respond to my own needs. Because I was scared of growing up. The specific causes of eating disorders are varied, but those factors are pretty common.

If experts really want to help those with eating disorders, they should look at why so many people are so unhappy; they should teach schoolkids how to talk about their feelings without resorting to masochism; they should look at why so many girls and women feel they ought to put themselves last; and, most of all, they should look at the causes of self-loathing as opposed to the manifestations of it.

But as even those without eating disorders know, it's hard to deal with complicated issues - far easier just to obsess about fashion models.

The Guardian, 19 March 2015
© Guardian News & Media 2015

Britain & its citizens

More than 80,000 children across Greater Manchester are living in families who have fallen behind with their gas or electricity bills

Rob Jackson

Energy companies need to show struggling families more warmth

SOME ISSUES:

Do you think energy companies should help people who are struggling to pay their bills?

As well as heat, what other services and items do people need to maintain basic living comfort?

Do you think other large companies should help out people who are struggling to make ends meet?

Who else should be helping those who are struggling?

My Canada-dwelling brother likes to joke about how rubbish our winters are compared with his adopted nation's apocalyptic snow and ice storms.

It's true - Greater Manchester's weather would be a little clement for Arctic foxes. But it's still cold enough to complain about, particularly in the last couple of weeks, and for some families the chill is no laughing matter.

Research by The Children's Society suggests that more than 80,000 children across Greater

Manchester are living in families who have fallen behind with their gas or electricity bills at some point. Families like these are often forced to choose between keeping their children warm and paying down their debt.

While carrying out our study on cold homes and energy debt, a mum-of-four whose house had no insulation or double glazing, told us: 'It can get so cold that when the heating isn't on you can see your breath.'

No child should be made to grow up in a cold, damp home...

The trouble is that too often parents have little choice but to turn the heating down, leaving their children without a hot meal, hot bath, or warm bedroom at night. The impact on their health is predictably miserable - kids living in families who have struggled with energy debt are three times more likely to become ill this winter.

As our report says, no child should be made to grow up in a cold, damp home that puts their health at risk because their family can't afford to turn the heating on and is living under the burden of energy debt.

That's not to say that bills should be avoided or left unpaid. But it's time energy companies stopped using aggressive and intimidating tactics to claw back debts from vulnerable families.

And it's about time suppliers worked with families to find workable solutions, including lowering or suspending debt repayments over the winter, when children's health is most at risk.

Another mum told us a debt collector from an energy company began 'banging down the door' of her house,

telling her 'we've got to turn your electricity off', while her frightened children looked on.

Instead of being offered the support she so desperately needed she was made to foot the bill for installing a pre-payment meter in her home, leaving her with even higher energy costs.

If that's enough to leave you cold why not join The Children's Society's campaign to get energy companies to show some warmth to vulnerable families this winter.

Further information:
www.childrenssociety.org.uk/warmth

Manchester Evening News, 7 February 2015

It's about time suppliers worked with families to find workable solutions

The Liverpool locals who took control of their long-neglected streets

Granby Four Streets in Toxteth is a rare success after New Labour initiatives drained the area of life - Oliver Wainwright

SOME ISSUES:

Who should be responsible for the condition of our streets and towns?

Why do you think these residents had to take the situation into their own hands?

Do you like the look of the area you live in?

Would you enrol your friends and neighbours to make changes if the council were not keeping the area nice?

With relentless rows of boarded-up windows, punctuated by half-demolished corner shops and purple shocks of buddleia sprouting from the rooftops, the streets of Toxteth in inner-city Liverpool present an eerie, post-apocalyptic scene.

It is the result, not of some great environmental disaster or mass industrial collapse, but of a series of failed regeneration plans since the 1980s, most recently New Labour's "Housing Market Renewal Pathfinders", that have drained the streets of all life, to make way for promised visions that never arrived.

But turn the corner on to Cairns Street, at the bottom of the Granby Triangle - where only 70 out of 200 homes are still inhabited - and a busy scene erupts into life, an oasis amid the desolation. A street market is in full swing, beneath a dense bower of trees and climbing plants, while trainee builders erect scaffolding across the fine redbrick frontages either side of the road.

After 30 years of neglect, the few remaining residents of the Granby Four Streets have taken the future of the neighbourhood into their own hands: they've established a community land trust (CLT), taken ownership of

"We were condemned... It was punishment for the riots. Bins weren't collected, streets weren't swept and a mythology built up"

the derelict properties from the council, and will have the first 10 homes refurbished by March.

"We never thought we'd see this day come," says Eleanor Lee, 65, who moved to the area in 1976 and has witnessed its progressive decline since the 1981 race riots, which saw buildings torched and 500 people arrested. "After the riots an invisible red line was drawn around the area - it was an unspoken policy of no maintenance and no investment. Once houses are boarded up it sends a signal."

"We were condemned," says Hazel Tilley, 59, who lives a few doors down. "It was punishment for the riots. Bins weren't collected, streets weren't swept and a mythology built up: people came here to buy their drugs or dump their shite."

Things began to change four years ago, when residents organised a guerilla gardening group to green the streets, with tubs and wild planting that have since won a Northwest in Bloom award, and began organising a monthly market, selling vintage clothes, cakes and Caribbean food. "It completely turned

the atmosphere around: now we had a pretty street that we could all be proud of," says Lee. "Even if it was still empty."

With the help of local housing campaigner Ronnie Hughes, they formed a CLT in 2011 and attracted funding from a Jersey-based social investor, Steinbeck Studios, to put together a plan for the area, drawn up by young London architecture collective, Assemble. With a track record of building temporary projects that have breathed life into abandoned sites with unusual beauty and wit - from converting a petrol station into a cinema, to making a performance space beneath a flyover - the practice has brought a fresh approach to how these empty homes could be rethought on the tightest of budgets.

"We want to retain the generosity and flexibility of the original buildings," says Assemble's Lewis Jones, pointing out how nearby pathfinder new-builds have much meaner windows and tighter space standards. "We're also celebrating the idiosyncrasies of what's already

After 30 years of neglect, a few remaining residents have taken the future of the neighbourhood into their own hands

"This might look ordinary, mundane and expected. But believe you me it's not.

When we all began this latest push four years ago, many people in positions to know told us we had no chance of ever seeing builders working on these houses again.

Well here they are, we are being widely supported and it is little short of a miracle to see them.

That's why I keep wandering around taking photographs!"

Ronnie Hughes, A sense of place blog

there: if a floor is missing, why not leave it out and have a double-height space? There isn't the usual pressure to extract the maximum possible value from the site and put profit before people."

A second phase of work, planned for the next street along, imagines a spectacular winter garden within the empty brick shell of a gutted house, as well as a new terrace to complete the other side of the street - which was bulldozed to make way for a plan that failed to materialise. The plans for the first 10 homes are kept simple, says Jones, and don't require wet trades in order to open up the process of construction to local young people. Five will be put up for market sale while the other five will be available for affordable rent to members of the CLT.

"I love Assemble's attitude," says Lee. "They're so bold and fearless in their designs, and they've worked so closely with us to interpret our vision. It's so different to how the housing associations operate."

The project, which is joint-funded by Steinbeck, central government's Empty Homes initiative and the Nationwide Foundation, represents a rare example community land trust in an urban context. Originally imported from the US, the model keeps the land in community ownership in perpetuity, with houses sold or rented at a rate that is permanently linked to local incomes. There are now over 170 such groups in the UK, mostly in rural areas due to prohibitive land values in cities, but a national CLT network was launched in July with a pot of £3m, to encourage their growth in urban areas.

"It's a tipping point," says Ann O'Byrne, Liverpool's cabinet member for housing. "The council has abandoned these people for the last 30 years and left them to fester. But now we've gifted the homes to the CLT and they're showing that this will be the place to live, right on the edge of the city centre."

"What's happening in Granby is an important prototype for northern councils, who've been so badly hit by the cuts," says Ronnie Hughes. "Two years ago, the whole area was nearly signed over to a private developer, but now the people who live here have finally got a formal stake in the place. It's an extraordinary achievement - and now it's extraordinary forever."

The Guardian, 27 November 2014
© Guardian News & Media 2014

All photos © Ronnie Hughes,
asenseofplaceblog.wordpress.com

Now we had a pretty street that we could all be proud of

Bullying

A letter to ... the child who is bullying my daughter

You don't get to see the tears that stream down my daughter's face when she tells me that she had a horrible day at school. Today you refused to work with her on a group project, saying: "Why do we have you? We don't like you. Why can't someone else be in our group?"

The tears when she is the last to be chosen for a team. The tears when she is the only one not invited to a birthday party. The questions she asks me - why isn't she as good as everyone else in the class and why is she always left out? What is wrong with her, she wants to know, that makes everyone so mean?

Maybe you just want to be like the others in your class and not stand out by accepting the child who is different to you; the child who is a bit chubby, who speaks another language, who dresses differently. Maybe your parents say things about our family. Maybe others say things that are mean and you join in with them.

But can you imagine how this little girl is feeling? She feels all alone and isolated in this world. She just wants to be friends and

In any other situation this would be considered abuse. Yet my daughter continues to suffer.

SOME ISSUES:

Have you known someone who was bullied? How did it make you feel?

Why do you think people bully others?

What should schools and communities do to help tackle bullying?

Should support be offered to the bullies or the bullied or both?

have fun with everyone. She hasn't done anything mean. But she can't understand why everyone is mean to her. Why everyone stops talking when she comes near them. Why she is never allowed to put forward her own opinion. Why others play games such as being the first to push her off the trampoline, or trip her up so she can't walk down the corridor.

While you may feel good about yourself by making fun of others, my daughter doesn't laugh any more. She doesn't joke or sing or be silly. Life for her is serious and cruel. She just wants to hide away from everything and everyone.

She went from being a good student to one whose head is so full of everything she has been through during the day that she can no longer focus on her schoolwork. She is the girl who wakes during the night with splitting headaches from thinking too much about what her life has become. She has black circles under her eyes as she can't sleep properly. Her only comfort is eating, which makes her put on weight.

It doesn't matter how much love and support we give her, every day she must return to the part of her life which makes her so desperately unhappy. You may think that you are just having fun, but this is destroying my daughter and her family. To watch her suffer every day is devastating. When the parents of the children and the teachers say that they cannot see a problem and "they are just being children", all I can say is that you are allowing the problem to exist.

In any other situation this would be considered abuse. Yet my daughter continues to suffer. I continue to hold her every day when she cries - it hurts so much as she can't understand what she has done to deserve such pain.

To the children who are bullying my child: is this what you planned to do? Or did you just not think about the person who is the target of the bullying - my daughter?

Anonymous

The Guardian, 10 January 2015
© Guardian News & Media 2015

> I continue to hold her every day when she cries - it hurts so much as she can't understand what she has done to deserve such pain.

Even as a young child, I can clearly recall my mother actively instilling in me that all people needed to be treated with love and respect. Making fun of those who are poor, look different, have different names or even pick their noses was simply unacceptable and I was to understand that this type of behaviour would not only hurt other people, but also bring my level of love and self-respect down. She made it a point to show me love and kindness, and to explain how peer pressure works and that no matter what, I needed to stand up for what's right. Deep stuff, right? Not really. It started from day one and it made perfect sense to me. Not complicated, just a matter of beginning early and leading by example.

I'm not a counsellor, a mental health professional or even a parent (yet). What I am however, is a crusader for love and active teaching through example about these issues that unfortunately exist in the lives of our children and loved ones. What I am, is an activist for those who were like me in the third grade, who weren't brave enough to stand up for themselves and who feared the disapproval of other people. I will continue to forgive those who treated me poorly (I still know each of them personally) and understand that they were not as fortunate as I was to have such a solid example about how unacceptable that behaviour was and is. I will continue to lead by example in the best way I can by expressing

Daffnee Cohen

I'm not a counsellor, a mental health professional or even a parent (yet). What I am however, is a crusader for love and active teaching through example

compassion, understanding and love to those who may be different from me.

I hope that others who read this and possibly even reflect on their own personal experiences move forward in a progressive way that sets a positive example for others. I invite you to actively teach your children, siblings, nieces whomever that bullying happens and more importantly, that it is our job to stand up and show

love to those who are being bullied as well as those doing the bullying. Bullying ends when we step forward and hold our social circles responsible for their words and actions and how those affect people around us. It also ends when we stop being passive about this awful social behaviour, step up and unite. To love, peace and happy confident children!

12 March 2015
www.daffneecohen.com

Disability

When seeing isn't believing

If someone sitting in a wheelchair suddenly stands up, what would be your first thought? Penelope Friday ponders on the danger of making assumptions

SOME ISSUES:

When you hear that someone is disabled, what sort of disability do you think that means?

What different conditions can disability include?

What can we do as a society to be more accepting of people with different disabilities?

People make assumptions. We all do it. From my faint surprise when I discover other women who are as passionate about football as I am, to the idea that if a baby is dressed in a pink onesie then it must be a girl, our ideas about how the world works are often based on unchallenged assumptions. People think they know what disability looks like. They've watched the Paralympics, seen disabled athletes. There's so-and-so's son down the road who was hit by a car and who walks with a limp. This is disability: we know it, we can see it. And that makes sense to people. People like to know where they are with something, and it's much easier to conclude that the world is divided into the people we can see are disabled, and all the other people, who are faking it.

It is this sort of attitude which led to a conversation on Radio 5 live a few weeks ago. Talking about tightening up the regulations surrounding mobility scooter use, the presenter, Nicky Campbell, asked his disabled interviewee: "Do you get angry when you see perfectly able-bodied people on a mobility scooter?" Clearly, this implies that you can see at once whether a scooter user is disabled or not: it implies that disability is visible. If you can't see it, it's not there.

A common assumption - but also a dangerous one. It is unchallenged beliefs like this which can, at their worst, lead to situations like the one in an Asda car park when a man ended up dead after an altercation over a disabled parking spot. Alan Watts called out sarcastically to Brian Holmes, who didn't 'look' disabled, "You look like you need a wheelchair". He then got out of his car to remonstrate further, eventually killing Holmes with a single punch. On a lesser scale, but still an important one, many people I know (including myself) have experienced disablist abuse based on the theory that they can't be disabled because their disability isn't visible.

There have also been the issues surrounding disabled supporters at the World Cup in

Essential Articles 2016 • www.carelpress.com

Brazil. It seems likely that some supporters did indeed have tickets meant for disabled people without being disabled, and that is horrific. But I would argue that the furore surrounding the situation has been blown out of proportion. It seems likely that other supporters used fake tickets to get into the stadia in general but this didn't cause such a fuss. And it also seems very likely that many of the so-called fakers of disability were, in fact, disabled. Shock, horror! Disabled people turn out to be disabled… no, there's not really much of a story in that, is there? You are far more likely to sell newspapers with righteous indignation about 'scroungers' and

why 'wheelchair user' has been preferred by disabled people. Firstly, I don't believe anyone spends 100% of their time in a wheelchair, which the phrase implies. Secondly, using a wheelchair does not necessarily mean that you can't stand up or walk at all. The language surrounding disability matters. It shapes viewpoints, and affects the general public's attitude and behaviour towards disabled people. With the BBC enforcing the idea that disability is immediately visible, and newspapers using inappropriate language, it is hardly surprising to discover that these sorts of attitudes are rife in the world around us.

Photo posed by model

if I stand up. I too could have my picture all over the internet with "FAKER" written in big letters beneath it. Similarly, I have a blue

It implies that disability is visible. If you can't see it, it's not there.

'fakers' – the 'in' language for describing people these days, it seems. Accusations have been running riot thanks to some people with wheelchairs standing up to applaud a goal.

It is noticeable, incidentally, that many of the newspapers (and not just the tabloids) have returned to the largely defunct term 'wheelchair-bound' to describe people in wheelchairs when covering this story. But there is good reason

But it means that many disabled people in the UK – indeed, I would suggest most disabled people – live in a culture of fear. Fear that anything they do or do not do will be used to 'prove' that they are faking disability, that they're "just lazy" or "trying to cheat the benefits system". As a wheelchair user who can walk a little, I'm always hyper-aware that someone is likely to think I shouldn't have the wheelchair

badge because my walking is severely limited (and always painful), but I look 'normal'. It could be me in that car park being killed because of someone's erroneous beliefs about what disability is or is not.

To **assume** might make an **ass** out of **u** and **me** — or it might lead to something so very much worse.

Disability Now, September 2014

Disney needs a princess with Down's syndrome

Why should one of my daughters be able to relate to Disney's plucky heroines, while my other one can't? Keston Ott-Dahl

SOME ISSUES:

Do you think the Disney princesses are positive role models for young girls?

Do you think there should be more variety of princesses?

Would a Down's syndrome princess be a good idea?

How else do you think people with Down's syndrome should be represented in society?

Would you sign this petition?

When I came into my living room expecting to see my daughters singing and dancing to their favourite movie Frozen, I was surprised to find Jules (my precocious six year old) sitting on the couch with tears welling in her eyes. Delaney, her 15-month-old sister was still sitting on the floor, her hands raised in the air and wiggling to the music, hadn't noticed her older sister had left her side.

"What's wrong Jules?" I came and sat down next to her.

She gained her composure after a few seconds then said, "Delaney can never be a Princess Mum."

"Silly, of course she can" I replied, initially not giving her concern much thought.

"No Mum, there are no Princesses like Delaney".

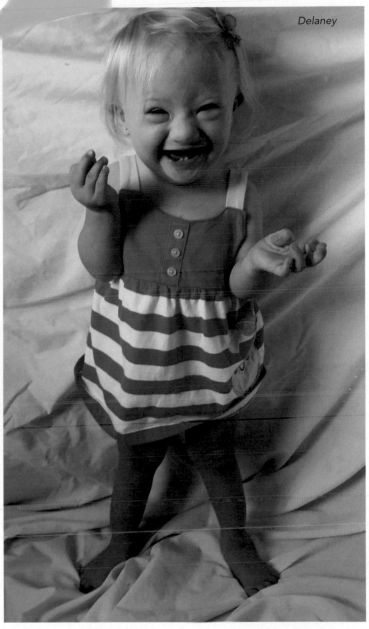

Delaney

But Jules was adamant, "No Mum, there are no Princesses like Delaney".

Jules, who is a beautiful blond haired, blue eyed girl, is a typical Princess by any Disney standard and so is Delaney, but with one big difference. Delaney has Down's syndrome. And I realised Jules was right.

My partner Andrea and I are already outspoken parent activists in the Down's syndrome community, but it took my six year old to recognise that her baby sister Delaney and people like her are excluded on even the most elementary level, even as children.

Andrea and I knew we had to do something, not just for Delaney but also for Jules.

My first thought was to call Disney. But realising that Andrea and I are two measly voices, we thought a petition would be a great way to get more voices to join us. We started the Care2 petition with an initial goal of 1,000 signatures. We had that in an hour!

"What if we get 10,000 signatures?" Andrea was shooting for the moon.

I agreed, "Now that would be something." We had the 10,000 signatures in less than a week. As of 30th October 2014, we have over 55,000 signatures and still have two weeks to collect more.

When we decided to save Delaney, which is a tale better left told in my memoir, everyone, including our families, was against the decision. Our families

> We started the Care2 petition with an initial goal of 1,000 signatures. We had that in an hour!

Keston, Andrea & Delaney

were concerned about our two other children (Jules and her 8 year old brother Jared), and how they would be treated by society and the attention that having a disabled child would take away from them.

Our families had valid, loving and thoughtful concerns; Andrea and I felt differently and chose to make our own decision even if everyone was against us and it was very hard.

Today looking at Jules I could not be a prouder parent and Andrea and I know that we were right in our decision. Both Jules and Jared are much more thoughtful and compassionate people because they love their little sister, who happens to have a disability. In this story, Jules is the real hero, and Delaney is her princess. I just hope that Disney can see this too.

The Independent, 31 October 2014
www.independent.co.uk

In this story, Jules is the real hero, and Delaney is her princess. I just hope that Disney can see this too.

LET IT GO...
The cold never bothered me anyway!

When Keston set up the petition, she hoped to get 1,000 signatures, however she got over 84,000 and counting!

To find out more about the petition, search 'Ask Disney to represent children with Down's syndrome in its animated movies' on the Care2 Petitions homepage: www.thepetitionsite.com

ABLE-BODIED ACTORS AND DISABILITY DRAG: WHY DISABLED ROLES ARE ONLY FOR DISABLED PERFORMERS

BY SCOTT JORDAN HARRIS

Able-bodied actors should not play disabled characters. That they so often do should be a scandal. But it is not a scandal because we do not grant people with disabilities the same right to self-representation onscreen that we demand for members of other groups who struggle for social equality.

Consider "Glee", a TV show unmistakably self-satisfied with its inclusiveness. Its makers would never have considered having Rachel, the female lead, played by a man in drag. They would not have considered having Mercedes, the most prominent black character, played by a white actress in blackface. But when they cast Artie, the main disabled character, they chose an able-bodied actor and had him sit in a wheelchair and ape the appearance of a disabled person.

These comparisons with blackface and drag may seem inflammatory or outlandish but those of us who make them (such as the actors who protested the casting of the recent "Ironside" remake) do not do so lightly or in order to bring cheap attention to our cause. We do it because the analogy is exact. To argue that it isn't is to argue that disabled people are less equal than others.

Women were once prohibited from performing onstage. The female characters in Shakespeare's plays were, in their first incarnations, played by boys doing their best impressions of women - and continued to be until society deemed this offensive, self-defeating and absurd.

Black and Asian characters were once often played by white actors. In "Tea House of the August Moon", Marlon Brando plays a Japanese man, with his eyes pulled tight across his face and his skin coloured yellow. Laurence Olivier was nominated for an Oscar for playing Othello in blackface. And Alec Guinness painted himself brown to play Prince Faisal in "Lawrence of Arabia".

Those actors observed black people and Asian people, and they tried to walk like them and talk like them. They used make-up and prosthetics to imitate their physical characteristics, and took roles that would have been

SOME ISSUES:

Do you think it is important to have disabled actors playing disabled characters?

When do you think this might not be possible?

Why is it offensive for an able-bodied person to play a disabled character?

What can be done to ensure greater diversity on our screens?

better played by black or Asian actors, two groups for which opportunities were already disproportionately limited. Today, just the idea of this is distasteful to us.

But able-bodied actors do all these things in efforts to imitate disabled people, and we do not protest. We are conditioned to be outraged when we see race being exploited onscreen. When we see disability being exploited onscreen, we are conditioned to applaud.

Just as non-white roles were once prized by white actors looking to show off their range, disabled roles are similarly prized by able-bodied actors today. A hundred articles and a thousand jokes have been written about how pretending to be disabled is a shortcut to an Oscar. For Hollywood stars, imitating disabled people in an effort to make able-bodied audiences think "Wow! I really believed he was one of them!" is a route to legitimacy as a serious actor.

The able-bodied narrative on this topic focuses on how "convincing" the performances of able-bodied actors are when they play disabled characters. To many in the disabled community, whether an able-bodied actor is convincing to other able-bodied people when playing a disabled person is immaterial. The ugly spectacle of it is fundamentally offensive.

When I see an able-bodied actor, even one as superb Daniel Day-Lewis, playing a great figure in the struggle for disability rights, such as Christy Brown in "My Left Foot", I feel the same way many black people would feel watching Day-Lewis play Malcolm X.

It wouldn't matter how great an actor Day-Lewis was, how expertly his black make-up was applied or how much he behaved like a white audience's idea of a black man. That he was onscreen in that role (and preventing a black actor from playing it) would provoke outrage. No-one would even begin to discuss whether he was "convincing".

The portrayals of disabled people that are considered the best, those that win Oscars for able-bodied actors, are often described as being "sympathetic" to disabled people. This

supposes both that sympathy is what disabled people are seeking from the able-bodied and that it is the best we can hope to get from a filmed depiction of our lives. We do not want sympathy. We want equality.

The idea of able-bodied actors giving performances that are "sympathetic" to disabled people also implies that the disabled community is not able to speak for itself, through our own actors, but must instead send out able-bodied envoys to speak to the world on our behalf via the cinema screen. There was perhaps a time when this was true, when using able-bodied actors in disability drag was the only way to get disabled characters onscreen. But that time was decades ago.

ACTORS IN DISABILITY DRAG WAS THE ONLY WAY TO GET DISABLED CHARACTERS ONSCREEN. BUT THAT TIME WAS DECADES AGO.

Now there are many disabled stars. RJ Mitte has cerebral palsy and brilliantly played Walter White Jr., a character with the same condition, on "Breaking Bad". Marlee Matlin's abilities are so prodigious she is the youngest person to win an Academy Award for best performance in a leading role, despite the disadvantages of being deaf and the roadblocks the film industry erects in the career paths of those with disabilities. Peter Dinklage won an Emmy and a Golden Globe for his work on "Game of Thrones" and stands out among its cast not because of his restricted growth but because of his expansive talent. There are many fine disabled actors. And there would be many more if young disabled people grew up feeling they had a fair chance to work in film.

The insurmountable irony of the focus on whether able-bodied actors are "convincing" in disabled roles is that, if we were truly concerned with convincing performances, no able-bodied actor would ever have been cast as a disabled character. When a hearing actress is cast to play a deaf woman, the majority of her performance is devoted to asking herself a stream of questions about deaf life in an effort to pass as a deaf person. When Marlee Matlin is cast as a deaf woman, those questions do not need to be asked. No viewer needs to be convinced Marlee Matlin is deaf. Her performance is automatically authentic.

Today, we find the sight of white actors portraying non-white roles in old films shocking. It often makes those movies unwatchably embarrassing. Years from now, films in which able-bodied actors play disabled characters will seem similarly misguided. They will be relics of a less equal age.

But the most important reason for casting disabled actors as disabled characters does not concern how films will be viewed in the future. It concerns how they are made now. Every time an able-bodied actor plays a disabled character it makes it harder for disabled actors to work.

Indeed, if we are okay with disabled roles being played by able-bodied actors, we are okay with disabled actors being prevented from acting at all. Able-bodied actors can play able-bodied roles. Disabled actors cannot. If disabled actors cannot play disabled roles, they cannot play any roles at all—and they are excluded from film altogether.

Articles are often written protesting, rightly, that there are too few roles in Hollywood for women in certain age ranges or performers from certain ethnic groups. For disabled actors the situation is even worse. Not only are there too few roles for disabled people but also, when those rare roles become available, they are generally taken by people who are not disabled at all. It's like casting the parts played by Meryl Streep not with Streep, or an actress like her, but with Harrison Ford in drag.

I know that last image seems ridiculous. It is ridiculous. It's ridiculous because women have a right to be represented onscreen by women. Just as people of colour have a right to represented onscreen by people of colour. And just as people with disabilities have a right to be represented onscreen by people with disabilities.

www.rogerebert.com
7 March 2014

THE UGLY SPECTACLE OF IT IS FUNDAMENTALLY OFFENSIVE

Education

Why I've taken my son out of school for a year...

Rather than send his five-year-old son to school, David Hurst has decided to give him a different kind of education, by travelling the world

SOME ISSUES:

Why might traditional school education not suit all students?

What might travel offer that school classrooms can't?

What do you think might be lost by not attending traditional education?

What could be done to enable more young people to benefit from travel?

Last year, my wife Debs and I came up with the idea for a family adventure with our two sons. A three-month, 7,500-mile trip, to forge family bonds and tick off some bucket-list locations before the children got stuck on the treadmill of education.

Before we set off, we had shown our then four-year-old son, Daniel, photographs of places we could visit. Debs and I were tremendously excited about the trip but to Daniel, we soon realised, it was largely incomprehensible, an abstract concept. To him, the places we were describing were just words. He asked a couple of questions, then wanted to get back to whatever it was he was playing with.

A short while later, when Daniel and his three-year-old brother Darley got to feast their own eyes on Stonehenge, Hampton Court Palace, the Angel

A door was unlocked, and suddenly they were hungry for as much information, as much history, geography and art as we could feed them.

of the North, Scotland's mountains and the Clifton Suspension Bridge, Debs and I couldn't answer their questions fast enough. A door was unlocked, and suddenly they were hungry for as much information, as much history, geography and art as we could feed them. Reading about the knights of old is all very well, but it's better if you can show your children where they lived.

When our journey took us to Spain (in a motorhome we bought after downsizing our Devon home) the boys' desire to learn continued, whether we were visiting Valencia or counting pebbles on the Andalusian coast. They picked up Spanish (and bits of other languages) at the campsites we stayed at en route. They were soaking up the world like sponges.

But we weren't just filling their minds with experiences. They were learning the value of exploration, that risk-

taking can be rewarding beyond expectations. And they were gaining rapidly in self-confidence. Even the greatest Oxbridge degree is worthless without an inner confidence to get out into the world and get stuck in.

We had a huge amount of fun, all of us, and our family bond grew stronger than ever on that trip. That's not to be underestimated: we didn't have children to not spend time with them. Yet family togetherness is something that gets lost in the maelstrom of modern life, too often forgotten in the race for a bigger house, nicer car, better job, or as we stare at a succession of screens, lost in our private digital worlds.

That wasn't for us. We wanted something different. Back home, we began planning another, bigger adventure.

Children in Britain have to be in full-time education by the term after their fifth birthday – but while education is compulsory, schooling is not. So a few weeks ago, we informed Daniel's (excellent) school-to-be that we'd be educating him ourselves until the start of the next school year.

We're piling into our Swift Escape motorhome once again, and will be travelling through Spain, Portugal, Morocco and more besides. We're also planning to fly to Australia. The idea is to continue what we

© David Hurst

They'll be interacting with people from all backgrounds, cultures and ages. We think this is important.

started on last year's three-month travels: we called it our Face2Facebook project and visited as many of our Facebook friends as possible, donating to charity for every one we saw. At the same time we will be broadening our children's horizons, opening our eyes to the wonders of the world.

Which is not to say the boys won't also be getting any traditional education. Being on the road means there'll be plenty of reading and writing time, but because we'll all be together we can seize the moments when Daniel actually wants to read, write

or do maths – so that he'll be more engaged and more likely to learn. And the teaching he and his brother get will always be one-to-one.

We're giving them something more too, which Debs and I call "education by astonishment". Our aim is to tailor our travels in order to show the boys somewhere astonishing for each of the National Curriculum subjects. Children are born curious, and new environments bring out that natural curiosity. Travel broadens education.

A criticism of taking children out of school is that they won't socialise with children their own age. It's true, Daniel and Darley won't find as many peers in the coming months as they would at school or nursery, but they will be socialising on a much broader scale. They'll be interacting with people from all backgrounds, cultures and ages. We think this is important – we want them to be able to get on with someone aged 90 from another country just as well as they can with a five-year-old down the road.

What my sons will learn this year is something that can't be taught in the classroom. Don't get me wrong, teachers generally do a first-rate job. But increasingly what we hear from teachers and parents is criticism of successive governments for making formal education a procession of tests, rather than a process that turns our children into confident, open-minded individuals.

So don't be surprised if you hear about more people doing what we're doing.

Daily Telegraph, 11 February 2015
© Telegraph Media Group Limited 2015

You can follow their family adventures via their blog: face2fb.wordpress.com Twitter: @DavidHurstUK and Face2fb Facebook page

SCHOOLS THREATEN TO INFORM POLICE IF STUDENTS ARE ALLOWED TO PLAY 18+ VIDEO GAMES AT HOME!

SOME ISSUES:

Is it the business of schools to control what happens at home?

Are there genuine reasons to worry about these games and their effect on youngsters?

If schools are concerned, how should they react?

What do you think the effect of this letter will be?

Parents of children in 16 schools have been sent a letter threatening to report them to the police if they allow their children to play violent video games such as: **Call of Duty** or **Grand Theft Auto**. The letter was sent to the parents of 15 primary and one secondary school in Nantwich, Cheshire, in response to reports from some children that they had played the games or watched adults play them.

The Headteacher who drafted the letter told reporters "We are trying to help parents to keep their children as safe as possible in this digital era. It is so easy for children to end up in the wrong place and parents find it helpful to have very clear guidelines."

Access to these games OR to some social media sites increases early sexualised behaviours (sometimes harmful) in children AND leaves them vulnerable to grooming for sexual exploitation or extreme violence.

Nantwich Education Partnership
Working together for all the children in Nantwich
To All Nantwich Education Partnership Schools
11 February 2015:

Dear Parents

Re: Computers, Tablets, X box Games and Social Media

All the schools in Nantwich work closely together with the Cheshire East Safeguarding Education Team to keep our children safe. We have received advice on the use of tablets, computers, X boxes and other digital equipment.

Lots of the children have had new technology/devices for birthdays and Christmas and seem to be enjoying playing a range of new games on them. There are some amazing apps, games and social media opportunities that our children are benefiting from. However, the local Safeguarding Team and school staff have serious concerns about some games and activities.

Several children have reported playing, or watching adults play games which are inappropriate for their age and they have described the levels of violence and sexual content they have witnessed:

Call of Duty, Grand Theft Auto, Dogs of War and other similar games, are all inappropriate for children and they should not have access to them.

Nor should they have Facebook accounts or interact on sites or media or messaging sites like WhatsApp that are not designed for their age.

Children should only play games or join social media sites that are rated suitable for their age.

We need to inform you all of the actions we are advised to take and why:

If your child is allowed to have inappropriate access to any game or associated product that is designated 18+ we will are advised [sic] to contact the Police and Children's Social Care as it is neglectful.

Access to these games OR to some social media sites such as those above increases early sexualised behaviours (sometimes harmful) in children AND leaves them vulnerable to grooming for sexual exploitation or extreme violence.

We know that parents expect us to keep their children safe so we look forward to your support with this issue. Schools will all be working with the children to help them understand how to keep themselves safe. If you would like to talk to anyone about your child's online or digital safety please contact your school; we are here to help.

Together we will keep this new digital world one of wonder rather than danger.

Yours Sincerely

Nantwich Partnership Headteachers

Source: www.audlem.org/newsroom/ nantwich-education-partnership.html

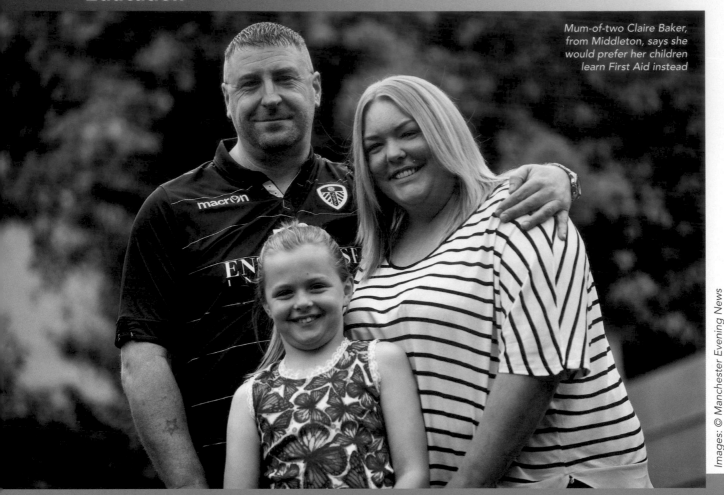

Mum-of-two Claire Baker, from Middleton, says she would prefer her children learn First Aid instead

Images: © Manchester Evening News

Atheist mum bans children from school trip to church and synagogue – and says she may stop them learning R.E.

Amy Glendinning

SOME ISSUES:

Do you think that students should have to learn about world religions?

Are there advantages to learning about religion even if you are an atheist?

Who should be responsible for deciding what students learn?

What subjects do you think are useful?

What subjects do you think should be taught at school?

Claire Baker, 32, says she believes an atheist upbringing is as much a choice as being brought up with a religion - which she does not want forced on her son and daughter.

Instead she would prefer her children Benn, 12, and Katie, eight, to learn first aid, because it would be more useful.

Claire says she feels the same way about all religions - and finds it offensive that people preach in public places or go door-to-door trying to convert people.

The mum is also considering removing her children from RE lessons at Elmwood Primary School in Middleton and Middleton Technology College.

She has refused to be a Godmother to a relative's child and says she believes people with no faith should not have to eat Halal or Kosher prepared food.

They can make their own minds up when they're older if they want to practise a religion

The mum spoke out after receiving a letter from the primary school about trips to places of worship.

She posted her comments about the school trip on Facebook - it provoked a huge debate - with some agreeing it is a parent's right to choose and others saying it is important to understand others' beliefs.

Claire, who lives with Benn, Katie, and partner Craig Livesey, 47, in Middleton and is a support worker for adults with learning difficulties, said: "From a young age I've always been an atheist.

"I chose non-religious schools for my children on purpose so they can make their own minds up when they're older if they want to practise a religion.

"I don't think RE should be on the curriculum - it should be replaced with First Aid, which is more useful in life.

"I was shocked to receive a letter for a school trip to a mosque, church and synagogue.

"I absented my child and have been debating for the best part of a year whether to take my children out of RE lessons.

"I respect that people choose to christen their children but I would also like them to respect that I have no interest in religion.

"Also why should I have to take my children to get baptised to get them into good schools? It's all about choice - I don't go banging on peoples' doors or preaching in town centres about it.

"People have accused me of being racist, but this is about all religions, not race."

The Manchester Evening News. was unable to contact Elmwood Primary School for a comment.

Current UK law states that all pupils should follow a curriculum which 'promotes spiritual, moral and cultural development' - of which RE is essential.

Government guidance also states the subject 'promotes community cohesion' and helps pupils 'become responsible citizens."

But parents are able to withdraw children from RE lessons.

The rules state:

"The use of the right to withdraw should be at the instigation of parents (or pupils themselves if they are aged 18 or over), and it should be made clear whether it is from the whole of the subject or specific parts of it. No reasons need be given.

"Parents have the right to choose whether or not to withdraw their child from RE without influence from the school, although a school should ensure parents or carers are informed of this right and are aware of the educational objectives and content of the RE syllabus. In this way, parents can make an informed decision.

"Where parents have requested that their child is withdrawn, their right must be respected, and where RE is integrated in the curriculum, the school will need to discuss the arrangements with the parents or carers to explore how the child's withdrawal can be best accommodated.

"If pupils are withdrawn from RE, schools have a duty to supervise them, though not to provide additional teaching or to incur extra cost. Pupils will usually remain on school premises."

Manchester Evening News, 25 May 2015

"I respect that people choose to christen their children but I would also like them to respect that I have no interest in religion."

10 things I Wish I'd known when I Was a teenage girl at school

With anxiety levels for teenage girls at an all-time high, Emma Barnett, a former stress-head, gives her younger self a good talking to

I am well-versed in the common refrain from older people around the school exam results-season: "Oh it was much harder in my day. These kids today don't know they've been born," or something to that effect, is how the highly predictable chatter goes.

However, these older naysayers couldn't be more wrong. The exam culture then, isn't what it is now. Nowhere near. And I definitely caught the tail end of it. I sat 11 GCSEs, four AS-Levels, three A-Levels and not to mention the endless mocks and internal school tests from the age of 11 onwards.

Exams punctuated my entire time at school. In fact I would go as far to say, they defined my entire secondary school experience. Yes I managed to enjoy other pursuits – namely a spot of drama, netball, tennis and fair bit of gossiping – but exams, or rather a fear of them, ruled the roost. And I had no idea until recently, how much so many of my friends had hated their school experiences because of their inability to get straight-A*s. They still talk of the 'shame' of getting As or even Bs and how the anxiety has haunted them into the world of work.

A new study showed teenage girls and middle-aged men account for most UK hospital admissions for people with stress-related illnesses.

Yes that's right: British girls, aged 15 to 19, are competing with men aged between 40 and 44, for who is the most stressed, according to the Health and Social Care Information Centre.

Moreover, experts have warned that an epidemic of anorexia is sweeping through the UK's top schools and that teenage girls from aspirational families are the "fastest-growing" social group using mental health services, in their bid to succeed.

In a nutshell our exam-obsessed schools, churning out hyper competitive children – addicted to comparing themselves to each other and the models of perfection served to them via the internet, are creating mental health time bombs.

SOME ISSUES:

Why do you think young people suffer from so much anxiety?

What sort of difficulties do young people face?

What can be done to help young people cope well with difficult situations?

If you could write a letter to prepare yourself for life as a teenager, what advice would you give?

Now don't mistake me, I think competition is very healthy. I think it's important to lose and have knocks, throughout your life. Doing badly or losing keeps you focused and energised. But something is seriously going wrong in Britain when our top schools need to introduce 'boasting weeks' and tests where no one can get full marks* so kids know it's OK to fail. And when teenage girls are neck and neck with middle aged men (most of whom probably have mortgages, their own children and money worries to stress about) in terms of their anxiety levels.

It is easy when you have left school and entered the world of work to scoff at the worries of teens – but we shouldn't.

... It is with this in mind that I have written a few pointers to my teenage self that I could have done with, when battling the spots, the revision, the hormones, the school bitches – but mostly for when I was beating myself up for not doing as well as I thought I could...

I have written a few pointers to my teenage self that I could have done with...

*Boasting weeks: girls were encouraged to reflect on their achievements and celebrate their successes to overcome their reluctance to self-promote.
Tests where no one can get full marks were intended to teach girls not to expect to be perfect and that they had the ability to handle failure and to bounce back

Photo posed by model

School systems are afraid that hormonal boys won't be able to control their eyes and minds... so they send girls home to change.

However, Lauren Wiggins tackled what she saw as the underlying issue in her letter to the Principal:

"Dear Sturgeon,

I have a concern I would like to bring to your attention. In today's society, a woman's body is constantly discriminated against and hypersexualised to the point where we can no longer wear the clothing that we feel comfortable in without the accusation and/or assumption that we are being provocative. This unjust mindset towards women is absolutely absurd.

"The fact that authority figures, especially males, can tell young women they must cover up their shoulders and their backs because it's 'inappropriate' and 'a distraction' is very uncomforting. Schools are the social building blocks in an adolescent's life meant to teach them how to communicate and develop relationships with others and also learning about themselves and who they want to be. It's preached upon us to be individual, to be ourselves.

"The double standard here is that when we try, we are then told we're wrong. We may not truly dress, act or speak how we want because authority figures, and I use that term very loosely such as yourself, tell us we can't. Yes, I understand there are restrictions to how much and how little of your body that shows, but that applies when people show up in their bikinis or bra and panties. Though I do believe women should legally be allowed to publicly be shirtless considering males are, it's mindsets like yours that keep that as something that is shamed upon.

"So no, Mr. Sturgeon, I will not search for something to cover up my back and shoulders because I am not showing them off with the intention to gain positive sexual feedback from the teenage boys in my school. I am especially not showing them to receive any comments, positive or negative, from anybody else besides myself because the only person who can make any sort of judgement on my body and the fabrics I place on it is me.

"If you are truly so concerned that a boy in this school will get distracted by my upper back and shoulders then he needs to be sent home and practise self control.

"Thank you, have a nice day."

UNIFORM DOESN'T SOLVE THE PROBLEM

Having a uniform does not keep a school free from controversy. A school in Bridlington, Yorkshire, is facing a backlash from parents for its attempt to prevent violations of its uniform policy.

The current uniform policy states: "Plain black trousers (no leggings, jeans, or 'fashion' trousers) or plain black knee length skirt for girls." The school is said to be considering banning girls from wearing skirts and insisting that all pupils wear one style of trousers with the school logo on them.

This is intended to solve the problem of pupils wearing too tight trousers and the embarrassment caused to male teachers who have to reprimand girls for wearing too short skirts. Predictably, the school is facing opposition from parents who oppose both the use of a single supplier for the trousers and a ban on skirts. Their petition. which has over 1,000 signatures states:

"We believe that this uniform change is penalising the whole school, for the misbehaviour of the few children that refuse to follow the current uniform rules."

Sources: Various

If you are so concerned that a boy will get distracted by my upper back and shoulders then he needs to be sent home and practise self control

Family & relationships

When parents split up –
your stories

**People were asked to share the moment they realised
their parents were going to break up. Here is a selection:**

Photo posed by model

A cruel choice...

Our mother took the three of us to Italy without Dad when I was 13. We stayed in a hotel with full board and went to the beach every day. It was quite wonderful and I don't remember asking why Dad had not come. One day at lunch, we were sitting at a table, my younger brother and sister on either side of Mum and me opposite. She told us they were getting divorced: Dad was moving out to be with his new girlfriend and would probably want to take one of us to live with them.

My little brother put his hand on Mum's arm and said: "Not me. I want to stay with you."

My sister put her hand on Mum's other arm and said: "He can't have me, I am staying with you, too."

Then all three silently looked at me. I felt for a horrid moment that they all hated me. But I was certain that Dad liked me a lot less than the other two. So I said: "Well, me, he won't want."

I wonder how my mother felt at that moment. We never talked about it again. In the end, he took none of us but he did take the dog, which hurt all of us kids the most.

Saskia Wesnigk-Wood

But I was certain that Dad liked me a lot less than the other two. So I said: "Well, me, he won't want."

SOME ISSUES:

Which personal account do you find the most moving?

Is there ever a good way for parents to split up?

What sort of support should be provided for parents and families to help them through difficult times like these?

Should parents ever stay together 'for the children'?

Dance of freedom...

My mother could have gone to university. She was a working-class London grammar school child and an avid reader. She loved rock music and was considered born out of her time. She got pregnant, aged 18, with me and married hurriedly in 1958. To her young eyes, my father had the look of Marlon Brando. "He was silent and broody and could look after himself," she said. She was a romantic then.

My father drank and gambled. He used his wife as a punch bag. He burnt her records on the coal fire. She hid books under the settee cushions. We "begged" potatoes from the next door neighbours. They were bemused but generous.

I was 10 years old, one of six, and my youngest sibling was one. I came home from school one day and was met by my mother at the kitchen door. "I'm divorcing your father," she said. She explained what this meant. Like a bird in first flight I was lifted up but without moving. We had a spontaneous dance around the kitchen. I still had my coat on. It was one of the highs of my childhood and family life.

I still see the pebble-effect vinyl on the kitchen floor when I remember. It was all, O Blessed Mother Mary, a welcome release.

Louie Robinson

Photo posed by model

Don't tell your brother...

When my mum and I left home 45 years ago, I was 11. She said one day, "We're leaving your dad. Don't tell anyone, not even your little brother. Just put any toys and books you really want to take in a pile over there." I didn't have a clue what was going on - 45 years ago, divorce was uncommon and no one I knew had divorced parents.

A few days later, she told me to let my teacher know she would be picking me up from school in the morning for a dental appointment. She collected me, leaving my little brother at school, and we went. She'd left a note on the kitchen table saying she was leaving and had made arrangements for my brother to be collected from school.

And that was it. We never had the big talk about how it wasn't my fault and Mummy and Daddy both still loved us, let alone why she'd just taken me and not both of us.

She had arranged to stay with an old school friend, where we slept on camp beds for a couple of months. I don't remember ever missing my dad, but I missed my little brother so much that first night.

Martin Murray

We never had the big talk... let alone why she'd just taken me and not both of us... I missed my little brother so much that first night.

Breeding flies and edible plastic: the kitchen of the future

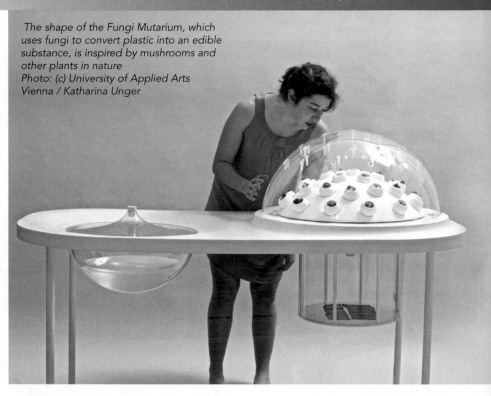

The shape of the Fungi Mutarium, which uses fungi to convert plastic into an edible substance, is inspired by mushrooms and other plants in nature
Photo: (c) University of Applied Arts Vienna / Katharina Unger

You might have heard of edible insects, but have you considered eating plastic? From 3D printed nutrients to smartphone-controlled mini gardens, this is the future of the humble kitchen

Rich McEachran

SOME ISSUES:

Would you consider eating insects?

If meat production is damaging to the environment, how important is it to seek alternative options?

Why is food waste a problem?

What can be done to reduce food waste?

Do the meals of the future sound attractive?

The kitchen of the future will be full of cutlery that cleans itself, Willy Wonka-style food pills and edible packaging, according to forecasting agency Trendstop. It also predicts that by 2063, fresh, organic produce will be in high demand and we'll be turning our backs on supermarkets to go hyperlocal and grow our own food.

So what are the future-thinking innovations that might influence how we produce food and what we do with our waste?

Food from flies

Katharina Unger, founder of Austrian collaborative design studio Livin, is one of a number of designers and startups who want to see the kitchen become more symbiotic with food production. To help achieve this, Unger has designed Farm 432, a device that allows people to grow their own protein source at home by breeding black soldier flies – the "432" refers to the number of hours it would take 1g of fly eggs to produce 2.4kg of larvae protein (equivalent to £22 worth of minced lamb from your average London butcher).

"Insects can totally disrupt the way we currently produce food", says Unger. "I wanted to enable people to take advantage of this and independently produce

Gender

This isn't an anti-feminist backlash - it's a brutal war on women, without rules

Wherever you look, women and girls are not safe, not thriving

Yasmin Alibhai Brown

SOME ISSUES:

Why do you think every country in the world suffers from gender inequality?

Why do women suffer more than men the whole world over?

Is there a connection between gender inequality in developing countries and developed countries?

What can we do to help tackle sexism and inequality in our own society?

My husband says a global war is being waged on women. He is right. What is going on in the East, West, South and North cannot be attributed to "the backlash" or a new "masculinism" or a reactionary fight back. It is a brutal war without rules or redress, beyond the reach of international laws or institutions.

Last week the BBC broadcast India's Daughter, made by Leslee Udwin, whose films include the much loved East is East. The documentary revisited the savage murder-by-gang-rape of the young student Jyoti Singh in Delhi in 2012. Five men were found guilty and sentenced to death. One hanged himself, the others have appealed. Udwin got permission to interview one of the rapists, Mukesh Singh, in prison.

Singh blames the woman and is unrepentant. "A girl is far more responsible for rape than

Benefits cuts have been catastrophic for impoverished women

HOW DARTH VADER DEFENDS MY DAUGHTER'S RIGHT TO BE A GIRL

It's fancy dress week at my daughter's preschool, because it's Halloween. So what should she go as? The question I should have asked my daughter was "What fancy dress would you like to wear?". However, what we actually asked was "Would you like to wear your Darth Vader costume?" I just couldn't let this opportunity to enlighten her peers slip by.

**Simon Ragoonanan
manvspink.com**

SOME ISSUES:

Why do you think our society has such strong ideas about what girls' clothes and boys' clothes are?

How might restricting what girls and boys can wear, affect their development?

Why should clothing be labelled as male and female at all?

What are the positive aspects of a more open-minded culture?

A local mum recently made a good point to me that I had never considered. Many of the children my two year old daughter goes to preschool with will be at the same primary school, in the same year, maybe even the same class. They may continue to be her closest peers until adulthood. The same goes for lots of the children we see at playgroup, at the local park, soft play, the library, or even just the high street. What these children think, how they perceive the world, how they treat my daughter, will have a massively influential impact on the woman she becomes.

Part of my approach to parenting is to constantly refer back to my memories of growing up, and use that to positively inform my approach. The fantastical worlds of comic books and Star Wars loom large in my childhood (and adulthood too). They fired my imagination, but perhaps more importantly provided both escapism and inspiration to make sense of the world in the darkest times of my youth.

I want my daughter to have access to all of this too. Luckily, superheroes and Star Wars are still very much in vogue.

It's also fair to say that I'm not a fan of Disney Princesses, and pinkification in general. So as well as simply sharing my enthusiasm for Star Wars with my daughter (she has all my old toys), this is also about me offering her an alternative to girly girl culture before she heads into the school system, and peer group pressure becomes a driving force in her development.

So far, my daughter really enjoys this stuff. So do all the little girls who come over for playdates – they always love to play with our Star Wars and superhero toys.

However, it is very clear that to the likes of Hasbro and Disney (who own Marvel and Star Wars) these brands are just for boys. That's another battle being fought by myself and others, but in the meantime, here in the trenches, our kids are forming opinions on what is and isn't for boys or girls, based on the way these brands are marketed.

As she grows older, I worry my daughter might be singled out for displaying an interest in this geek stuff, simply because she's a girl. I don't want her to be perceived as 'weird' because she's a geek. Perhaps even teased, ostracised, or bullied.

This mentality starts young. One time, a little boy saw me with my daughter, looked unsure, then asked me: "Is she a boy or a girl?". When I confirmed 'she' was in fact a girl, he countered "Then why

Image © Simon Ragoonanan
manvspink.com

is she wearing a Spider-Man t-shirt?". "Because she likes Spider-Man." I replied. The boy's older sister then chimed in, "Yeah, girls can like Spider-Man too y'know!". The boy went away with a new concept to contemplate, while hopefully this exchange supported his sister's seemingly healthy outlook on gender.

It also exists in adults who should know better. A friend who recently became a dad asked me 'Why are you trying to make your daughter into a boy?'. Grasping for a calm answer, I replied 'I'm not. There's nothing inherently male about any of this stuff. I think whatever she wears are girl's clothes, her toys are girl's toys, her books are girl's books. Because she's a girl.' After mulling it for a moment, he agreed with me. This had never occurred to him before, but now it makes sense.

My daughter and I get so many positive comments from parents when we're out and about. I often then hear them telling their son or daughter how cool my daughter looks. Perhaps we are influencing some parents too.

WHEN I CONFIRMED 'SHE' WAS IN FACT A GIRL, HE COUNTERED "THEN WHY IS SHE WEARING A SPIDER-MAN T-SHIRT?".

I am confident I am doing right by my daughter, that these things are a positive influence on her developing personality. But in order for her to not be socially excluded because of it, I also need her peers and their parents to accept girls can be just as engaged with these things as boys.

So I feel that each time she runs around with a cape, carries her cuddly Spidey to the playground, wears her beloved Batgirl dress yet

again, or goes out dressed as Darth Vader, she is doing her part to challenge (some) people's idea of what it is to be a girl.

My hope is that by the time she gets to school, and her attire will switch from geek chic to school uniform, her fellow pupils will be so used to the idea that girls can like this stuff too, that it won't be weird at all.

23 October 2014
http://manvspink.com

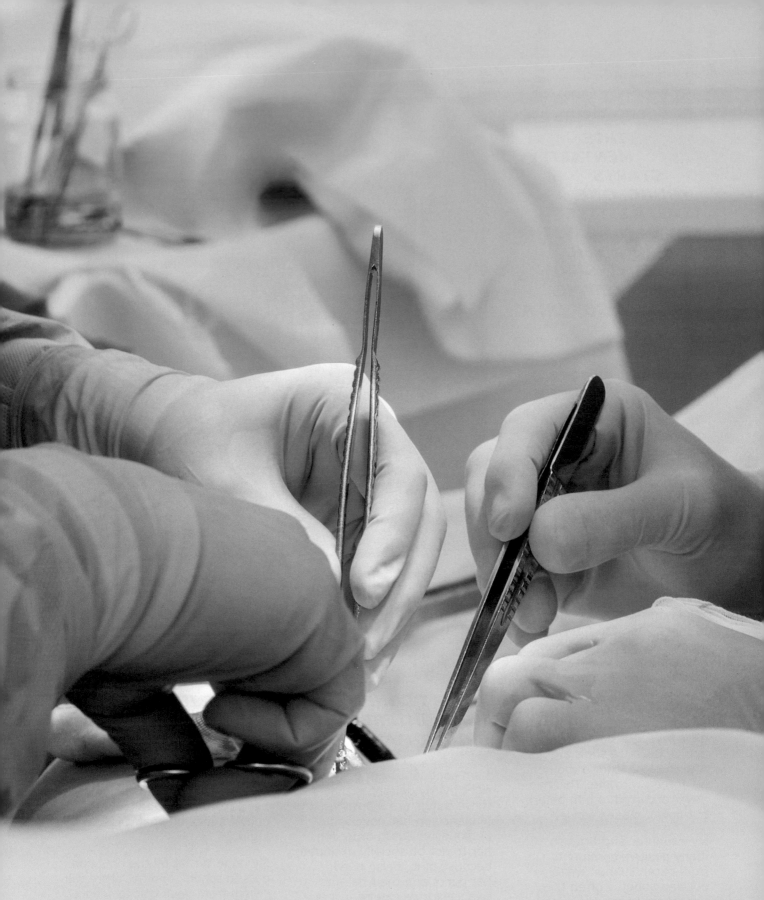

Health

I fell under a moving train in India

Gabrielle in Kenya a few days before she arrived in India and had the accident
© Gabrielle Jackson

It was bad enough finding myself with a train hurtling over me, inches above my face. But what I did after that was even more stupid - *Gabrielle Jackson*

SOME ISSUES:

Do you think it is safe to go travelling alone?

What should the writer have done following her accident?

Why do you think some people want to travel so much?

Would you ever put adventure before your own health and safety?

When I was run over by a train in Mumbai and thought I was about to die, my first thought was: "How could I do this to my mum?"

My second thought was about kebabs.

It's funny how a near-death experience makes you realise what's important.

It was March 2012 and I had come to India in search of a good kebab. In fact I'd arrived there only a few hours before.

For most of the previous seven months, I'd been travelling around the Middle East, eating meat on a stick as research for a book I planned to write about my search for the best kebab in the world.

People told me I was mad to travel to all those "dangerous" countries alone on my kebab quest ("Iran! Lebanon! Georgia! You can't go there - something terrible might happen!") On the other hand, nobody suggested it was dangerous to stop over in India for a few weeks on my way home to Australia.

And yet there I was, underneath a moving train.

I'd been running along a platform trying to get on a train with a German tourist I'd just met at my guesthouse. She jumped on the train as it took off, but I struggled in my flip-flops to reach the door in time to hop on.

My first thought was: "How could I do this to my mum?" My second thought was about kebabs.

I have no memory of what happened next. All I remember is waking up to hear people yelling: "Don't move! Stay still!"

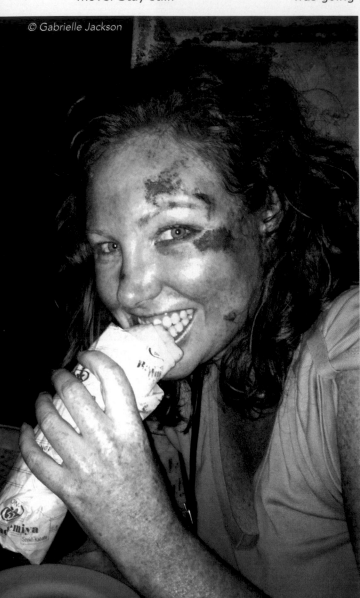

© Gabrielle Jackson

I didn't know where the voices were coming from or if they were talking to me, but on the off chance they were, I remained still.

It was as I made that decision that it dawned on me I'd been in an accident. I recalled a sensation akin to being in a tumble dryer, but it wasn't until I opened my eyes that I had any idea of what was going on.

There, about 20cm from my face, was a train hurtling over the top of me.

The tumble dryer sensation had been my body ricocheting back and forth between the train and the platform. Somehow I had fallen into the gap between them and landed flat on my back.

I lay still, trying to figure out if I was dead or alive. I don't know how long I was lying beneath the train, but I know that the whole time I was there, I was waiting to die. I imagined a ladder hanging down from the end of the train taking my head off.

Then the train was gone and I was alive.

People in the crowd on the platform at Andheri station said I was a miracle, that I had good karma.

After I'd been lifted from the tracks, people wanted to touch me. A woman was asking me questions, holding up fingers, ringing my guesthouse on her mobile phone. She asked me if I could walk.

"Where's my other flip-flop?" I asked.

"Stop talking about your shoes! I'LL BUY YOU ANOTHER PAIR OF SHOES!" she said.

I gathered it wasn't the first time I'd mentioned my missing shoe. My major concern was that the ground seemed a bit dirty and I didn't really fancy walking on it barefoot. Her major concern was that I'd lost the sight in my right eye and broken a hip, and possibly my right shin and right shoulder.

Her incessant questioning about my sight made me reach for my face. When I felt the liquid, I looked down at my body for the first time. There was blood all over me.

What happened next still doesn't make much sense to me. I went to the hospital to have the wounds cleaned on my face, shoulders, elbows, knees, hip and ankle.

But then, against the advice of a doctor, I left without x-rays or a CT scan, clutching only a supply of painkillers and antibiotics. "I've had broken bones before," I kept repeating. "I'm fine."

Of course I wasn't fine. When I thought about that train steaming over my head, my heart pounded and sweat leaked from every pore. At those times, I couldn't figure out if I was alive or dead, and at some point I decided that India was a pretty good place to be if you wanted to figure that out.

For the next three months, then, I continued to travel around India, without telling my family or friends at home what had happened to me.

I decided not to think about the accident. I'd think about that once I'd figured out all the meaning-of-life stuff.

That worked out OK until the tourist friends I'd met only hours before the accident, and who had looked after me like lifelong friends in the wake of it, had to leave.

It was about three weeks after the accident, on my first day alone, that I began to experience severe headspins. I awoke one morning to my room spinning out of control. I clutched the side of my bed to make sure I was still on it and not falling.

At first I refused to acknowledge it had anything to do with the accident, and Googled "iron deficiency" since I'd not been eating much meat. None of my symptoms matched an iron deficiency but I bought iron tablets anyway.

When the dizzy spells got so bad that I felt seasick every morning, I went to see a doctor in a suburban GP clinic in Goa. It turns out post-traumatic vertigo is common

When I tried to do yoga there, the instructor told me my shoulder was seriously injured and yoga was a terrible idea.

I went to a different class, but I couldn't do any of the poses that involved shoulder movement, which was most of them. All my other wounds had healed, but not the shoulder. I still couldn't lift it three months after the accident. I was still walking around with my forearm at right angles to my upper arm. I still couldn't wear shirts unless they buttoned up, or tie my hair back or do any action that required lifting my right arm above waist level.

That's when, finally, I figured it was time to go home, time to tell my family what had happened and have the shoulder x-rayed.

But not immediately.

Instead I booked myself on a 10-day silent meditation retreat run by a Burmese monk in Thailand. It was a

Also, I would not have had to undergo surgery to fix the many problems that had developed because of my decision to leave the hospital without having any x-rays all that time before.

None of this seemed very amusing during the many months of painful physiotherapy that followed. Even now, although I can swim, dress myself and do my hair in a ponytail, I still don't have a full range of movement.

My family and friends couldn't understand why I hadn't told them, or why I left the hospital without having tests. All I could say was that it felt easier to deal with the pain than consider the fragility of life.

Looking back on it all now, I can see there are some lessons in all this, but very obvious ones that shouldn't have required a near-death experience:

All I could say was that it felt easier to deal with the pain than consider the fragility of life.

after a head injury and the symptoms typically start three weeks after the impact.

The doctor sent me for an MRI scan to make sure the vertigo was the extent of my head injuries. It was almost as terrifying as being run over by a train. Thankfully, I got the all clear. My brain was OK, or at least recovering. What the MRI couldn't tell me was if it was the head injury, or the shock, that made me act in complete denial about what had happened to me.

In any case, my denial wasn't over. Instead of addressing my ongoing shoulder pain I booked myself on a flight to Rishikesh, India's spiritual heartland.

dreadful experience. I have never put my body or my brain through so much pain. Sure, there might be some benefits in learning to stop your brain whirring 24 hours a day, but to do that while sitting on a hard wooden floor for 10 hours a day while nursing a painful shoulder is probably not advisable.

At last I returned to Australia and had an x-ray. It turned out my shoulder was broken.

If only I had had the x-ray at the time and immobilised the shoulder properly by way of a sling, it would not have been so completely immobile more than four months later.

- Never run in flip-flops.

- If doctors tell you to get scans or x-rays, get scans or x-rays!

- Don't take life too seriously. OK, I almost died, but I didn't. And despite the insanity of this episode, it did make me realise that it was quite simple pleasures that make me happy in life: good conversations, meals shared with interesting people and working at a job I believe in.

Gabrielle Jackson now lives in Sydney where she works as the deputy opinion editor for Guardian Australia.
The Guardian, 11 February 2015
© Guardian News & Media 2015

Stretchers lining the corridors and unbearable crowding: The reality of life working on the front line of the NHS

Our A&E departments are stretched to breaking point

Bernadette Garrihy

SOME ISSUES:

Do you think doctors and nurses are respected in our society?

How much do you think medical staff should get paid?

Why do you think the hospital staff are so overworked?

How do you think the government can help hospitals to run more effectively?

I've come on duty for my 8am shift in A&E. Before I even walk through the door, I see five ambulances outside the emergency entrance, and my heart sinks. This usually means the A&E department is completely full and there's no space to offload new cases. Sure enough, as I walk the draughty corridor into A&E, it is lined with patients on ambulance stretchers, eleven of them in total, most of them elderly.

At the head of this line is Winnie, a fragile lady of 83, wrapped in a colourful crocheted blanket, dozing fitfully in spite of the noise and bright lights around her. Sister in charge greets me with a grim look; Winnie has already spent more than four hours on the ambulance stretcher. Thankfully the A&E doctors and nurses have already examined her, diagnosed a chest infection and started antibiotics via a drip, but there is still no room in the inn. All cubicles in the department are filled with patients who are waiting for beds on the wards, but news from the early morning bed-meeting is that there are no empty beds anywhere around the house.

Until ward rounds begin and discharges occur, we must continue to care for all the patients in our overcrowded department and continue to accept more. "We just can't keep all of these patients safe in such conditions," sister says, and I'm genuinely shocked to see tears in her eyes. She's worked in A&E for thirty-four years and is as tough as they come.

As A&E nurses and doctors, we tend to be a resilient lot; we thrive on the high pressure, the fast pace, the variety of patients and cases. I have a moment to reflect on how the relentless nature of working in A&E is "turning and burning" (turning off and burning out) so many colleagues, before the emergency doors slide open again, and another ambulance stretcher is wheeled in to take our queue up to an even dozen.

It's another elderly patient, who had a "funny turn" over his breakfast this morning. His carer called NHS 111, who advised calling for an ambulance and attending A&E. (In fact, 1 in 6 calls

"We just can't keep all of these patients safe in such conditions," sister says, and I'm genuinely shocked to see tears in her eyes.

made to NHS 111 results in a visit to A&E). This poor old chap suffers from advanced dementia. He is clearly distressed, shouting and trying to get off his stretcher. There's no way that I can leave him like that for what may be hours, so I quickly get the history from the ambulance crew, examine him, get an ECG (in the corridor- there's no place else) make a phone call to his

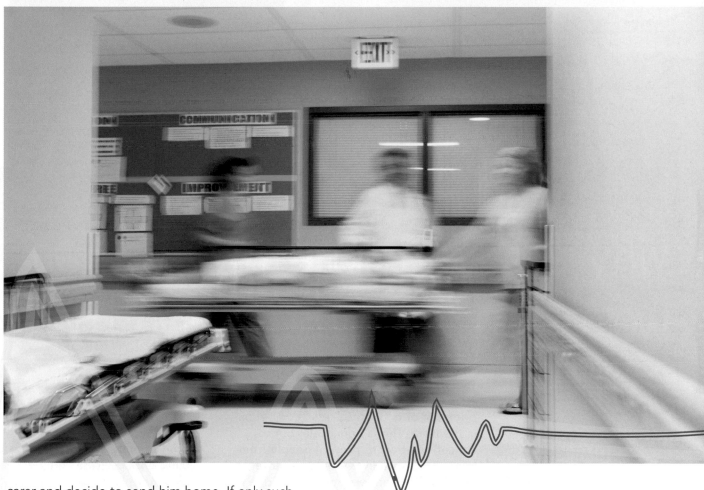

carer and decide to send him home. If only such patients had access to better care plans in the community. His visit to hospital has done him no favours whatsoever.

I finally make it into the main part of the department. The registrar who has been on duty overnight is waiting to hand over a department filled with 68 patients. Our normal capacity is for just 32.

He looks weary. The shift has been short a doctor overnight (in spite of being advertised at premium locum rates) and the overcrowding in the department has been unbearable. For him it's the last of a set of nights he says have been

"the worst of my career". I might take this with a pinch of salt if I didn't know that this chap is also an army medic, and has literally practised in war zones.

I take handover from him, tell him to be careful driving home and get ready to see the next patient in the queue. As I do, Winnie is finally moved from her ambulance stretcher to a hospital trolley. She now joins a new queue for a bed on the ward. It's only taken her five hours.

Dr Bernadette Garrihy is an A&E consultant in the West Midlands.

The Independent, 6 January 2015
www.independent.co.uk

Efforts to prevent suicide must take into account some apparently paradoxical differences between men and women

Daniel Freeman and Jason Freeman

Photo posed by model

Why are men more likely than women to take their own lives?

SOME ISSUES:

Why do you think more women than men consider suicide?

Why do more men than women actually end their own lives?

Why might gender affect emotional and mental health?

Are men encouraged to talk about their emotions and feelings?

Where can men go for help?

What can we do to help men who are considering suicide?

This week saw the deputy prime minister, Nick Clegg, appeal for the widespread adoption of a "zero suicide" campaign in the NHS. This is admirable, but a concerted effort to prevent people from taking their own lives would be more effective if we understood why suicide is a particularly male problem. It's known as the "gender paradox of suicidal behaviour".

Research suggests that women are especially prone to psychological problems such as depression, which almost always precede suicide. In western societies, overall rates of mental health disorders tend to be around 20-40% higher for women than for men.

Given the unequal burden of distress implied by these figures, it is hardly surprising that women are more likely to experience suicidal thoughts. The Adult Psychiatric Morbidity in England 2007 survey found that 19% of women had considered taking their own life. For men the figure was 14%. And women aren't simply more likely to think about suicide - they are also more likely to act on the idea. The survey found that 7% of women and 4% of men had attempted suicide at some point in their lives.

But of the 5,981 deaths by suicide in the UK in 2012, more than three quarters (4,590) were males. In the US, of the 38,000 people who took their own lives in 2010, 79% were men.

(These are startling figures in their own right, but it is also worth remembering just how devastating the effects of a death by suicide can be for loved ones left behind. Studies have shown, for example, an increased risk of subsequent suicide in partners, increased likelihood of admission to psychiatric care for parents, increased risk of suicide in mothers bereaved by an adult child's suicide, and increased risk of depression in offspring bereaved by the suicide of a parent.)

So if women are more likely to suffer from psychological problems, to experience suicidal thoughts and attempt suicide, how do we explain why men are more likely to die by suicide?

It's principally a question of method. Women who attempt suicide tend to use nonviolent means, such as overdosing. Men often use firearms or hanging, which are more likely to result in death.

In the UK, for instance, 58% of male suicides involved hanging, strangulation or suffocation. For females, the figure was 36%. Poisoning (which includes overdoses) was used by 43% of female suicides, compared with 20% of males. A similar pattern has been identified in the US, where 56% of male suicides involved firearms, with poisoning the most common method for females (37.4%).

Less is known about the choice of methods in attempted suicides that don't lead to a fatality. A European study of over 15,000 people receiving treatment after an attempt did find that men were more likely than women to have used violent methods, but the difference was less pronounced.

Why do methods of suicide differ by gender? One theory is that men are more intent

on dying. Whether this is true remains to be proven, but there is some evidence to back up the idea. For example, one study of 4,415 patients admitted to hospital in Oxford following an episode of self-harm found that men reported significantly higher levels of suicidal intent than women.

Another hypothesis focuses on impulsivity – the tendency to act without properly thinking through the consequences. Men are, on the whole, more likely to be impulsive than women. Perhaps this leaves them vulnerable to rash, spur-of-the-moment suicidal behaviour.

Not all suicides are impulsive, of course, and even for those that are, the evidence is mixed: some studies have reported that men are more susceptible to impulsive suicidal acts; others have found no such thing. What we do know is that alcohol increases impulsivity, and that there's a clear link between alcohol use and suicide. Studies have found that men are more likely than women to have drunk alcohol in the hours before a suicide attempt, and that alcohol problems are more common in men who die by suicide than in women.

The third theory is that, even in their choice of suicide method, males and females act out culturally prescribed gender roles. Thus women will opt for methods that preserve their appearance, and avoid those that cause facial disfigurement. Again, the evidence is patchy. But a study of 621 completed suicides in Ohio found that, though firearms were the most common method used by both sexes, women were less likely to shoot themselves in the head.

Clearly much work needs to be done before we arrive at a reliable picture of what's going on here. But it is striking that suicide, like mental health in general, is a gendered issue – it sometimes affects men and women in radically different ways. That's a lesson we need to take on board in research, clinical care and prevention efforts alike.

The Guardian, 21 January 2015
© Guardian News & Media 2015

Follow @ProfDFreeman and
@JasonFreeman100 on Twitter

If you are having suicidal thoughts, contact the Samaritans. Helpline 08457 90 90 90 (24-hours)

14% of men and 19% of women had considered taking their own life.

And women aren't simply more likely to think about suicide – they are also more likely to act on the idea.

7% of women and 4% of men had attempted suicide at some point in their lives.

But of the 5,981 deaths by suicide in the UK in 2012, more than three quarters were males.

'My son wanted to die; we begged for help but there was none'

After a number of suicides among people let down by NHS mental-health services, one family tells Anna van Praagh why things must change

When Linda Jones received a call from her distraught husband, one cold day in December 2008, to say that their beloved 17-year-old son, Matthew, had committed suicide in his bedroom, she was inconsolable, as any mother would be. But she was not surprised.

Matthew, who died from asphyxia, had been chronically depressed since he was 13, and had attempted suicide before.

In the weeks running up to his death, Mrs Jones, 61, a former civil servant, and her husband, Roger, also 61, a barber, who lived in Thornton, near Blackpool, had kept him under almost constant supervision, so frightened were they for him. They had begged the authorities for help, believing their son should be sectioned for his own safety. But, despite the chronic nature of Matthew's mental illness, they felt abandoned and let down.

The despair the Joneses feel at the state of Britain's mental-health services is becoming ever more prevalent. Only last week, we heard the harrowing story of Kim Lindfield, a 27-year-old charity worker, who committed suicide on a ward at Wythenshawe Hospital, Manchester, after a catalogue of missed opportunities in her care.

It was also reported that the health service ombudsman found that Stephen Foster, 48, a Norfolk author who committed suicide days after being discharged from hospital, had been "let down" by the two NHS trusts. Trezza Azzopardi, his partner, the Booker-shortlisted novelist, described the hospital trust's behaviour as "arrogant, dismissive and shambolic".

Then there was the harrowing story of Jacqueline Wilson, 42, a mother of three, who killed herself in Accident and Emergency in hospital in Lancashire last month after being left alone in a side room, despite her distressed state and history of suicide attempts.

The statistics make equally disquieting reading. According to recent research by the Mental Health Policy Group, mental illness accounts for 23 per cent of the total impact of ill health but only gets 13 per cent of the NHS budget. The number of beds for mental-health patients has fallen by 8 per cent since 2011, according to a Care Quality Commission report, and last year, 236 young people with mental-health problems were placed in police cells because of a shortage of beds.

Even more are treated miles from their homes because of

Despite the chronic nature of Matthew's mental illness, they felt abandoned and let down.

chronic shortages of beds for in-patient care.

"The psychiatric system is in meltdown due to the long-term relentless agenda to close psychiatric beds to save costs and treat everyone, however severely disturbed or in crisis, under the care of already overstretched and demoralised community home-treatment teams," says Marjorie Wallace, chief executive of the mental

health charity Sane. "It is no coincidence that the suicide rate has more than doubled for patients being treated by these teams in the last few years. At Sane, we witness daily the impact of the failures of the psychiatric services on patients, families and front-line mental-health professionals. In many places, it has led to a situation which is both cruel and inhumane, with

He told us he was being bullied at school and that he was self-harming. We were horrified – completely distraught.

unnecessary suffering on all sides."

Mrs Jones saw at first hand the desperate situation facing people with mental-health problems. "The first time we had any inkling there was a problem with our son was one winter's morning in 2004, when Matthew was just 13," she says. "We were getting ready to take him to school and he just flew into Roger's arms and completely broke down, clinging to him and

terrible hallucinations, where he thought walls were closing in on him. He'd scream and shout in terror. He had regular panic attacks. The only way I could calm him would be to lie on the floor with him and hold him as he wept."

When Matthew was 15, he attempted suicide but told his mother what he had done. He was taken to hospital and referred back to CAMHS.

A few months later, his

night and I was terrified he was going to commit suicide. He started to say he couldn't go on, he couldn't stand school. In the day, he would go to his room and just sob. I'll never forget the sound of it. It was heartbreaking.

"I kept asking for a counsellor for Matthew, but we couldn't seem to get a straight answer from anyone, and felt we were just being passed from pillar to post. Then we were told that, at 16, Matthew was going to be transferred to adult mental-health services so we should wait to deal with them."

236 young people with mental-health problems were placed in police cells because of a shortage of beds.

sobbing. He told us he was being bullied at school and that he was self-harming. We were horrified - completely distraught."

Their GP referred Matthew to Child and Adolescent Mental Health Services (CAMHS), where staff said they would be in touch to arrange an appointment.

After four months, Matthew was much worse, regularly tearful and withdrawn and continuing to self-harm, but, despite calling them endlessly, Mrs Jones had heard nothing from CAMHS. In despair, she took Matthew to the centre in Blackpool to demand an appointment.

He saw a consultant who put him on anti-depressants and arranged a fortnightly session with a counsellor. "My little boy was very ill and very frightened," says Mrs Jones. "He was suffering from

consultant retired and his counsellor left for another job. Despite Mrs Jones begging for Matthew to be assigned another counsellor, she was told he wouldn't be, with no explanation. At each quarterly consultant session, he would be seen by a different locum doctor.

"Once, Matthew asked one of the locums, 'Which drugs am I on?'" remembers Mrs Jones. "The doctor just didn't know. Matthew said, 'How can you help me when you haven't even bothered to look at my notes?'"

Matthew's behaviour was becoming increasingly frightening. Once, he disappeared from school and came back hours later, having lacerated his neck and face with a knife. "Roger and I were beside ourselves - we didn't know what to do," says Mrs Jones. "I didn't dare sleep as Matthew was often up in the

After the transfer, things went from bad to worse. At an assessment in 2007, he was told they thought he had only mild depression and would need to find his own counsellor because they had a two-year waiting list. He stopped taking his medication, and because he was now classed as an adult, his new consultant said there was nothing they could do.

His parents were also told they would no longer be informed about his care because of confidentiality laws.

In October 2008, when Matthew was 17, he tried again to take his own life. After he was discharged from hospital, Matthew was admitted voluntarily to Parkwood Hospital in Blackpool for adult in-patient mental care. "The atmosphere in that place was harrowing," remembers Mrs Jones. "Matthew was by far the youngest person there, and it was a completely inappropriate environment for someone his age. He was terrified of the other patients, and didn't dare leave his room.

It was incredibly noisy and overcrowded, and Matthew only saw a doctor once in the six days he was there."

Back at home, he withdrew further into himself, spending more time in his room. "He frequently said he wanted to die," says Mrs Jones. "One night he sat on the floor and grabbed my ankles, tears rolling down his face, and begged me to help him die. Can you imagine how it feels to hear your son say that? Words can't describe the agony I went through."

It transpired at the inquest that just days before his death, Matthew had told his GP he planned to commit suicide and how he was going to do it. Alarmed, the GP had called the mental-health services, who visited the house while Mrs Jones and Matthew were out.

They did not tell Mr Jones why they had called, and when they telephoned the next day, a health worker told Mrs Jones she thought Matthew was "playing games".

"A few days later, my little boy was dead," says Mrs Jones, her voice cracking with emotion. "We had begged for help, begged for more support. But none was forthcoming. Matthew shouldn't have been left at home by that stage, he was a very ill young man who needed professional help."

Barbara Taylor, an academic whose book, The Last Asylum, describes her time as a patient in one of the last Victorian mental-health asylums, Friern Hospital, formerly known as Colney Hatch, in north London, believes that the problems in the system stem from the abrupt switch in the Eighties

"I kept asking for a counsellor for Matthew, but we couldn't seem to get a straight answer from anyone"

to the care-in-the-community model.

"The principle of reliable, effective care has been undermined by so-called 'community care' that basically means providing people with medication and little else," she says. "People are being left to deal with their own problems with increasingly restricted resources. The crisis is such that in-patient care is now almost entirely devoted to people who have been legally detained, so there is no longer a place for people seeking voluntary care.

"I don't mourn the closure of the old Victorian asylums, but I do feel sad about the complete failure in treating mental illness in this country through a highly flawed community-care model."

Sue Moore, of Lancashire Care NHS Foundation Trust, says: "The death of Matthew was tragic, and our continued thoughts are with Linda and her family.

"Whilst we are unable to comment on individual cases,

the trust has worked hard over the number of years to improve access to its services, and in particular the transition from CAMHS to adult mental health services. Following any tragic incident such as this, the trust undertakes a full investigation and subsequently implements any improvements that can be made to ensure high standards of care are reached and maintained."

Mrs Jones is a publicly elected governor on the Council of Governors of LCFT, who try to raise awareness of mental-health issues, is alarmed that since her son's death, she is not seeing any improvements in the way mental-health patients are treated.

"I'm constantly watching children like Matthew being failed by the system, just like he was," she says. "I feel so frustrated because things haven't changed. If anything, due to funding cuts, they've got worse."

Daily Telegraph, 7 February 2015
© Telegraph Media Group Limited 2015

Where to find help:

Papyrus is the national UK charity dedicated to the prevention of young suicide . If you are or someone you know is suffering from depression and needs help, call the Papyrus helpline on: 0800 068 4141; text 07786 209697; or email pat@papyrus-uk.org

'I FEEL LIKE I'M DYING'

THE EFFECTS OF PANIC ATTACKS AND ANXIETY, AND HOW TO OVERCOME THEM

CLAIRE EASTHAM

Come on, you can do this. Just keep it together. You've been practising all night, you'll be fine. Why haven't they arrived yet? This room is too small. Oh God it's happening again. Heart is racing and chest is tight. I won't be able to speak, I'll faint, I'm going to run around the room screaming and then everyone will realise what a freak I am. I have to get out of here now.

That is the day I walked out of a job interview, one which I really wanted, minutes before it began. I had (what I now know) was a panic attack, the worst of my life.

By definition a panic attack is a sudden rush of physical and psychological symptoms. In reality it's like having liquid terror injected into your veins. You cannot think straight and you have an overwhelming sensation that something is very wrong.

From an evolutionary perspective they are an extension of the fight or flight defence mechanism that helped humans to survive. In prehistoric times, cavemen relied on this rapid ability to react to danger. If a caveman encountered a hungry lion then he had two options; either fight it or run away. Both of these require huge surges of adrenalin to flood the body with the extra strength needed. The stress felt when he believed his life to be in danger triggered the fight or flight response.

Unfortunately the world has changed faster than evolution could adapt. These days, there is little chance that you'll bump into a lion at work, (unless you're Bear Grylls!). However, what if other things cause high levels of stress such as board meetings, interviews and heavy workloads? The brain is tricked into believing that the body is in danger and triggers the fight or flight response. The problem is, you can't actually fight your boss or run out of a meeting. So this extra adrenalin becomes redundant and instead courses through the body without an exit, causing physical symptoms such as a pounding heart and sweating.

The brain, unable to recognise any present danger, becomes distressed by this reaction and asks questions, what is happening? Why am I reacting like this? This in turn increases the adrenalin and the vicious cycle continues, otherwise known as a panic attack.

There are many arguments as to why and how panic and anxiety develops in a person: genetics, difficult childhoods, trauma, but there is no concrete evidence. What's important is to understand them and learn how to manage the effects.

SOME ISSUES:

Have you ever experienced any of the symptoms of a panic attack?

How can people help those suffering from an attack?

Who is responsible for making sure people understand how to help those suffering from an attack?

THE STRESS FELT WHEN HE BELIEVED HIS LIFE TO BE IN DANGER TRIGGERED THE FIGHT OR FLIGHT RESPONSE.

SO WHAT DO PEOPLE NEED TO KNOW ABOUT PANIC ATTACKS?

THEY CANNOT HURT YOU

It might feel as though you're about to die or lose your mind, but you're not. It is also very unlikely that you will faint. Panic attacks are a strong dose of fear and this causes both the body and brain to react intensely. Try and think of them as a trick. You are not in any real danger, but you feel afraid. For example, in the cinema when watching a horror movie you can feel scared even though you're perfectly safe. Try and think of panic attacks in a similar way.

DON'T BLAME YOURSELF

Panic attacks are an irrational reaction and therefore cannot be treated in a rational way. Arguing with your thoughts or berating yourself to snap out of it will only make it worse. Instead, try and accept what is happening and be kind. Make yourself comfortable in whatever way you can. Try and get some fresh air, listen to some music and do some steady belly breathing to increase the oxygen flow.

ASK FOR HELP

If you find that they are disrupting your day to day life and preventing you from doing certain things; dining out, going to the supermarket, or speaking in meetings, then it might be time to get some help. Both anxiety and panic attacks are very treatable and there are numerous dedicated charities such as Mind and Anxiety UK which can offer help and advice.

1 IN 4 OF US

Most importantly, they are much more common than you think. In fact one in four people have experienced anxiety or panic attacks. So you are not alone. People are also a lot more understanding than you might expect - there is nothing to be ashamed of. Mental health is something that employers must take seriously.

For information on panic attacks: www.anxietyuk.org.uk

Claire Eastham's blog : http://weallmadhere.com

The Independent, 13 April 2015
www.independent.co.uk

Law & order

'I'm a big, strapping bloke. Who would believe I was a victim of domestic abuse?'

Male victims of domestic abuse are 'less visible and given less priority', according to a new report. Two survivors tell Theo Merz why this needs to change

"Some victims of domestic abuse are not identified as regularly," reads a line several pages into a new report from a UK domestic violence charity. "Particular groups of victims may be less visible to services or be given less priority."

Along with people from black, Asian and ethnic minority backgrounds, "male victims" form one of these neglected groups, according to the SafeLives study, which was published on Wednesday.

Perhaps this is unsurprising, given that the vast majority of SafeLives' 35,000-strong database of survivors is female. When we think of domestic abuse it is generally as a women's issue, while most high profile awareness drives, such as The White Ribbon Campaign, are aimed at reducing male violence against women.

But domestic violence against men is far from a niche concern. The most recent Crime Survey for England and Wales estimated that around 800,000 men – five per cent of the male population – had experienced domestic abuse in 2011-12, compared to 1.2 million women – or seven per cent of the female population. Since about 2005, around 40 per cent of domestic violence victims have been male.

And when these victims are not identified in time, the results can be disastrous. In this week's SafeLives report, titled Getting It Right First Time, the charity claims: "The impact of domestic abuse on the victim and on children – even once they have achieved safety – is severe and long-lasting."

SOME ISSUES:

Why do you think domestic violence is so prevalent?

What can be done to help victims of domestic violence?

How can we help to stop the cycle of domestic abuse within families & relationships?

Do we as a society offer enough support to male victims?

What can we do to make sure male and female victims get the support they need?

'I didn't think of it as domestic violence'...

Simon* is one man who understands the consequences of abuse better than most. For most of his 17-year marriage, this 47-year-old was subjected to domestic abuse from his wife, from having hot drinks poured over him to dinner plates smashed over his head.

While his wife was never physically violent towards their three children, she would often attack him in front of them.

"I didn't think of it as domestic violence and I think that's often true for male victims," he says now. "You put it down to mood swings. There was also the pressure of thinking that if I walked away, I might get a raw deal when it came to custody of the children.

"One day, though, my youngest children replicated her behaviour. They came into the kitchen and smashed a plate over my head - I got really angry, shouted and I remember them looking so shocked. They didn't realise it was wrong because this is what they had seen their parents doing. I wondered whether I was really protecting any of them."

He reached breaking point one night after his wife threw him out of the house - something she had done several times before. Simon, who was then working for the church and had never talked to anyone about the abuse he had suffered, went to speak with a superior in the church hierarchy.

"They said, go back to your wife and nobody will be any the wiser, but I knew I could never do that."

Since leaving the marriage, Simon has become involved with charities like the Mankind Initiative, which provides support for male survivors of domestic abuse.

"People are used to the idea of domestic violence being something that men do to women"

"It's a long battle to change people's perception," he says. "People are used to the idea of domestic violence being something men do to women, but when it happens the other way round, they can't get their heads round it.

"Going to the authorities was never an option for me. I thought, who would believe me - a big, strapping bloke? I can look after myself in that sense.

"But as a boy, growing up, I was always told that boys don't hit girls. That was the most important thing. It didn't matter how I was provoked, I would just never do that. So I would let her anger burn out rather than ever retaliate."

He says that men in similar situations should remember they are not alone and - if they feel unable to talk to anyone about the abuse - keep a journal and read it back, so they can get a more objective view of what is happening to them.

"Start thinking about ways out, too. You might hope that things will change but the reality is they never will."

> "Going to the authorities was never an option, I thought, who would believe me?"

> "I don't deny that more females are victims of domestic abuse, but it's a crime that can affect anyone"

"Why would you, as a man, put up with that?'

Ian McNicholl, 52, is another male survivor of domestic abuse. He was subjected to a 14-month ordeal by his ex-partner which saw her pour boiling water over him, put out cigarette butts on his face and genitals and attack him with a hammer.

He still bears the physical and psychological scars from that relationship, and needed his septum replaced after his ex assaulted him with a metal bar. The police became involved after McNicholl confided in a neighbour that suicide was the only way he could see out of the relationship.

His girlfriend was found guilty of grievous bodily harm and assault, and was sentenced to seven years prison time, but is now out on licence.

"When I tell people about what happened, some of them still ask: why would you, as a man, put up with that? It's because they don't understand how manipulative some people's behaviour can be - it takes all you have, until you've got nothing left.

"I don't deny that more females are victims of domestic abuse, but it's a crime that can affect anyone. The media need to give male victims more coverage and a more balanced view of what domestic abuse is."

*name has been changed

Daily Telegraph, 26 February 2015
© Telegraph Media Group Limited 2015

'Turing got a pardon. I want one, too'

Enigma codebreaker Alan Turing was posthumously pardoned for gross indecency, but thousands of British men's lives are still blighted by similar charges. Their primary offence? Being gay.

Mike Pattenden

You don't need a spoiler alert before being told how the Oscar-winning film, The Imitation Game, ends: mathematician and war hero Alan Turing was prosecuted for homosexual acts and, two years later, took his own life. In 2013, Turing was granted a posthumous royal pardon, but there are many more men whose lives were destroyed because of their sexuality, and who have lived with criminal records since.

The film inspired Matthew Breen, editor-in-chief of gay publication The Advocate, to set up a change.org petition demanding a pardon from the British government for 49,000 men convicted of consenting same-sex relations under the "gross indecency" law, 15,000 of whom are thought to be alive. A full-page advertisement in the Guardian in January, paid for by the movie's producers, the Weinsteins, and signed by Benedict Cumberbatch and director Morten Tyldum, helped propel the pardon49k.org petition to over half a million signatures; it was delivered to Downing Street the day after this year's Oscar ceremony by Turing's family.

James Taylor, head of policy at Stonewall, says "There are still thousands of men out there who face difficulties because of convictions on their records," Taylor says. "The fight for gay rights is not over." This is one story.

Stephen Close, 52, Salford

SOME ISSUES:

Do you think people prosecuted under this old law should be pardoned?

Why is it important to pardon people when laws have changed?

Do you think that enough has changed in society to make LGBT people equal?

Would you sign the petition that has been set up?

I joined the army in 1980 because I was confused about my sexuality. Coming from a deprived, working-class area, we had no education about things like that. I thought the army might make a man of me.

I was sent to serve in Berlin, where one of my jobs was guarding Rudolf Hess. He was one of the architects of the Final Solution, which included the imprisonment and murder of thousands of gay men. Ironically, a month later I was myself in a British prison for being gay.

I was 20 and I'd had a few drinks with another soldier one night. There was some chemistry there. We started kissing, but unbeknown to us, another soldier was watching. The following day I was on the firing range when two military policemen arrived. I was escorted back to camp, where they put the allegations to me. I denied it. After several days of constant questioning, I cracked. At that point, I was charged with gross indecency and sent for court martial. There was a lot of abuse from other staff and I was beaten up. All my army friends turned their backs on me. I suppose they were afraid. It was horrible.

I had no legal representation at the court martial. I was sentenced to six months in military prison and discharged with disgrace. I was then flown out of Berlin under armed escort and transferred to Colchester military prison,

I served four months. It wasn't long, but I was in pieces

where I had to wear red ribbons on my uniform to signify my crime, so the guards could keep an eye on me. My mum and dad came to visit me in prison. They were very understanding, really.

I served four months. It wasn't long, but I was in pieces. I broke down on the train home to my parents - it felt like my life was in tatters. I spent a lot of time in my old bedroom. I had suicidal thoughts, low self-esteem and no confidence.

When I was released, my father gave me a talk. He said: "Although we don't have much money, we will find a way of paying for a cure." I told him there was no cure and I had come to terms with what I am. My father embraced me and told me he still loved me.

Because of my record, I found it very difficult to get any decent work. I'd left a good job as an apprentice engineer to join up, too. In 2007, I had a job with a cleaning company and worked my way up to a supervising role. They won a contract to clean the local police stations, but that meant a criminal record check. I was told they wouldn't give me clearance. I had to explain why to my manager and hand in my notice. I was angry and hurt again.

Then, in January 2013, two police officers came to my house demanding I go to the station to give my DNA or I'd be arrested. My mum was frantic, asking to know what I'd done wrong. It turned out to be part of Operation Nutmeg, in which criminals with convictions predating routine DNA collection could have theirs taken and added to the national database.

Afterwards, I sat in my car, devastated. All the life was sucked out of me. I couldn't believe it was still haunting me after 30 years. Then Peter Tatchell launched a campaign and the DNA was destroyed. I applied to have my criminal record

Stephen Close: 'I served four months. It wasn't long, but I was in pieces.'

erased shortly afterwards, and eventually received a letter from the MoD saying my army record was now clear. There was no apology. It took a very long time to trust anyone, though I did go on to have two long-term relationships.

Now I want a pardon and an apology. Turing got one from [Prime Minister] Gordon Brown, but no one else has. It ruined my life. I have a poor job as a caretaker, no savings and no pension. I'm 53 and it's too late to start a new career. All for a kiss.

The Guardian, 28 March 2015
© Guardian News & Media 2015

Now I want a pardon and an apology... I'm 53 and it's too late to start a new career. All for a kiss.

Photo posed by model

Why wasn't more done?

When the UK was rocked by reports of horrific, widescale and long-lasting abuse of young girls by groups of men in Rochdale, Oxfordshire, Rotherham, Oldham and Derby we rightly asked how this could possibly happen.

What happened to many of the child victims is too awful to describe but what is known is that they, and their families, have been let down by the agencies that were meant to help them and by the wider society.

What do we mean by sexual exploitation?

SOME ISSUES:

Why do you think the young people who were abused were in such vulnerable positions?

Who is responsible for making sure all young people are safe?

What is leading groups of men to such abusive behaviour?

What should we do as a society about the attitudes shown by people who should have helped?

The definition

The phrase refers to young people under the age of 18 finding themselves in a situation or a relationship in which they are bribed, persuaded, coerced or forced to take part in sexual acts. Those exploiting these young people are in a position of power over them in some way - they may be older, stronger, more intelligent or have some social, personal and/or economic control. There may be violence or threats of violence involved, as well as grooming to give the impression of a caring relationship.

The young person is often vulnerable and, once involved, has a very limited amount of choice. Sometimes the victims have been so successfully groomed and manipulated that they are unable to recognise their treatment as abuse.

The victims have been so successfully groomed that they cannot see their treatment as abuse.

The law

Child Sexual Exploitation is not an offence in itself. The men convicted in Oxfordshire, for example, were found guilty of a total of 24 separate offences including rape, conspiracy to rape, rape of a child under 13, arranging prostitution, trafficking, sexual activity with a child under 13, sexual assault of a child, procuring a miscarriage and supplying a Class A drug. These were only a fraction of the crimes committed; what was inflicted on the victims was nothing short of torture.

The prosecution's opening speech in the Oxfordshire case summed up this horror:

"The depravity of what was done to the complainants was extreme… The facts in the case will make you uncomfortable. Much of what the girls were forced to endure was perverted in the extreme."

The grooming process

The victims

The men actively targeted vulnerable young girls from the age of about 11 or 12. They deliberately looked for children who were already at risk or out of control. Their targets were those in care or with troubled family backgrounds. A significant number of victims had already experienced neglect and/or sexual abuse.

As girls in Manchester explained: *"They go for the girls with the rubbish family lives because they know they will get away with it."*

They groomed their targets by giving them gifts or simply by showing them the care and attention that they craved. To quote the Oxfordshire prosecution lawyer again: *"The attention lavished on the girls at the outset was of course entirely insincere as it was merely a device to exploit their vulnerability. Having secured their confidence the men would ply the girls with alcohol and introduce them to drugs."*

Because the girls were already vulnerable and often already known to the authorities as 'troubled', they were easy to abuse, reluctant to approach agencies for help and unlikely to be seen as innocent victims.

The boyfriend model

The perpetrators often started by pretending to be attracted to the girls. An older man would introduce a young girl to a 'party' lifestyle, which involved sex. Having money spent on them, being made to feel special and cared for, a sense of drama and excitement, the thrill of doing something on the edge and the prestige of an older 'boyfriend' all add to the attraction for the girls at first.

In the next stage of the process the 'gifts' include alcohol and drugs - beginning the pattern of physical and psychological dependency which would be a important means of keeping the victims locked in to their dire situation.

Victims from Oxfordshire explained:

"Suddenly the guys were bringing me stuff. They said how lovely I was."

"They made me trust them for months, and I was their friend. I was flattered."

"The Asian men felt they ran Oxford. That was exciting. People were afraid of them. I felt protected. People respected them."

Becoming dependent

The abusers slowly separate a girl from positive influences in her life, making her more dependent on her abuser. They persuade her that she is loved, special, that she can only trust the person who is actually planning to exploit her:

"I know he really loves me" … (about a perpetrator convicted of very serious offences against other children).

"He may have other girlfriends but I am special…"

This grooming can be so convincing that the victims actually try to protect their abusers. In Manchester, one girl did not report abuse because there was a child's car seat in the car and she was worried that he had children who this might affect.

They are kept further hooked in by their dependence on alcohol and drugs. One of the Oxfordshire girls said:

"I wouldn't have done this if I was sober. That's why the men gave us so much to drink"

Violence

Control is then escalated by real and threatened violence. An Oxfordshire victim said:

"I was expected to do things - if I didn't they said they would come to my house and burn me alive. I had a baby brother."

The girls were taken to a variety of places where they were forced to have sex with other men who paid the abusers for what was, in fact, rape. The exploitation was intentional, persistent and organised. The girls were guarded and were beaten and burnt if they resisted.

Why wasn't action taken sooner?

Lack of experience

One reason that this level of abuse went undetected was that it was simply beyond the imagination and experience of people who should have been able to help. Social workers, teachers and police literally could not understand or believe what was happening. One social worker said: *"Even now I still can hardly believe that adult males would do what they did to children."*

The victims' background

The Oxfordshire review studied the case notes of six girls, vulnerable individuals who were said to live "within a culture of acceptance of very early sexual activity."

Ann Coffey MP heard from people in Greater Manchester that in some neighbourhoods child sexual exploitation had become the new social norm. Girls told her about unwanted approaches on the street:

"I get approached all the time when I am in school uniform." and "It's got to the point where men come up and touch us and try and get us into cars ... nobody came up and said what is happening?"

They did not report the harassment because they did not think anything would be done to help to stop it.

A Manchester youth worker spoke of a widespread mistrust of authority:

"The young people I work with do not trust anyone. They are frightened of being seen to be a snitch or grassing someone up."

How the authorities failed

Not believing the victims

The Rotherham report is scathing about the response of the authorities:

"...collective failures of political and officer leadership were blatant....Within social care, the scale and seriousness of the problem was underplayed by senior managers...Police gave no priority to Child Sexual Exploitation, regarding many child victims with contempt and failing to act on their abuse as a crime."

This is how the Oxfordshire victims saw it:

"If a perpetrator can spot the vulnerable children, why can't professionals?"

"No one believes me, no one cares"

"Why would a 13-year-old make it up?"

Many professionals at first failed to see the girls as victims and as children. What they saw instead was badly behaved girls making bad choices.

The language used in early reports reveals the attitude towards the girls:

"...believed to be prostituting herself... to pay for drugs."

"Deliberately puts herself as risk as she goes off with older men that are strangers."

At first the police regarded the girls as 'undesirables' who were not worthy of police protection.

Not recognising the abuse

Some agencies followed the girls' example and referred to their abusers as boyfriends. This meant that the age difference between the men and the girls was not recognised and also gave the impression of a consensual relationship, which was very different from the reality.

The police failed to make connections, for example when two vulnerable girls were found at the same address a week apart. Attempts to investigate were not sustained, shared or passed up the hierarchy.

Not taking action

Because it was difficult to obtain enough evidence to prosecute, particularly when the victims did not cooperate, police gave up on cases that they felt were hopeless, where with hindsight, they might have been able at least to disrupt the organised activities.

Why weren't the abusers prosecuted?

No precedents

The details of these cases were some of the most harrowing and difficult that police, social workers and teachers would ever have faced. Processes were not in place to deal with the nature and the scale of the crimes.

Refusal to cooperate

There were practical difficulties in dealing with the victims and obtaining evidence.

The families of the victims often distrusted authority because of previous encounters. As one Manchester boy put it, social workers *"just take you off your mums."*.

There were many examples of victims refusing to be interviewed or to make statements, refusing to identify perpetrators, demanding that no action be taken on their behalf, and sometimes criticising any action that was taken.

Fear and threats

Fear that no one could protect them and misplaced loyalty to their exploiters made the girls appear uncooperative, hardened and streetwise.

They separate a girl from positive influences and make her more dependent

The threats were real too. In Rotherham, one child who was being prepared to give evidence received a text saying the perpetrator had her younger sister and the choice of what happened next was up to her. She withdrew her statements.

Lack of evidence

There was often no realistic prospect of conviction. If a victim aged 13 looked 16 or older, and if she might say that she consented to sex, the Crown Prosecution Service would not proceed because no offence is committed if the child is aged between 13 and 16, and the adult could reasonably believe the child was 16 or over.

The court system

Victims who were brave enough to testify were faced with the ordeal of facing hostile questioning. One child in Oxfordshire who was prepared to give evidence in a 2006 trial withdrew from the case (leading to its collapse) in the face of what was to her a brutal and humiliating defence cross-examination.

In the Manchester report a victim of child sexual exploitation spoke about her treatment in court:

"It was like one attack after another. One of the barristers was not even asking me questions; he was just shouting at me... he kept asking questions that he was not supposed to ask."

Racial dimension

In all the areas involved, by far the majority of perpetrators were described as 'Asian'. The Rotherham report spoke about *"nervousness about identifying the ethnic origins of perpetrators for fear of being thought racist"* and a fear of playing into the hands of racists which may have had an effect on the investigation. In Oxfordshire, however, there was *"no evidence that the ethnic origin of the perpetrators played a part in the delayed identification of the group."*

What next?

No one disagrees that something must be done to stop the abuse which, we are told, is continuing in most towns and cities. All the reports contain long lists of recommendations and progress has been made since the initial investigations. Perhaps the change is most likely to come from acting on just some of the proposals contributed by the victims and their parents to the Oxfordshire report:

- However difficult they may appear, children need to be treated as children.
- Ask if they are ok.
- Start with the basic assumption that what the child says is to be believed.
- Signs of drug and alcohol use at a very young age are not normal and need real inquiry.
- Signs of physical harm must always be investigated.
- If you have any suspicions that a child may be being abused, do not be frightened to ask them about it ... and keep asking.
- Go with your instincts if something seems wrong.

In most cases the authorities were slow to act because they focused on the victims and their families rather than the exploiters. This was combined with an inability to grasp the nature of the abuse.

As one parent said, *"No service had the language, understanding and tools to acknowledge it, yet alone deal with it."* That's an excuse that can no longer exist.

The report on incidents in Oxfordshire noted: *"One does not need training in Child Sexual Exploitation to know that a 12-year-old sleeping with a 25-year-old is not right, or that you don't come back drunk, bruised, half naked and bleeding from seeing your 'friends'."* We may still need to ask what is wrong with our society if such common sense and humane attitudes need to be spelled out.

Sources:
Independent Enquiry into Child Sexual Exploitation in Rotherham 1997-2013, published August 2014.
Real Voices, Child Sexual Exploitation in Greater Manchester, published October 2014.
Serious Case Review into Child Sexual Exploitation in Oxfordshire, published March 2015

Too many of Scotland's women end up in jail - and that's bad news for us all

Jim Murphy

Imprisoning low-level female offenders does not reduce crime - it just makes nomads of women and children

SOME ISSUES:

Do you think criminals with children should be treated differently?

Does it make a difference if it is a mother rather than a father who is jailed?

What might be a better way to rehabilitate a criminal, other than prison?

What are the negative aspects of separating parents who commit crimes from their children?

Scotland sends too many women to jail. Two-thirds of female inmates are mothers. The status quo just doesn't work for the women, their children or society.

I am as uncompromising as the majority of Scots when it comes to crime; I want to see serious criminals punished. But we need to think about the impact jailing women has on their families. For too many children across Scotland, the imprisonment of their mother leads to the trauma of sometimes unnecessary separation.

It's a startling fact that today we send twice as many women in Scotland to jail as we did when the Scottish parliament was first established in 1999. Many jailed women have suffered from abuse and have mental-health problems. Many also have alcohol and drug problems.

When a father goes to prison in Scotland, 95% of children remain living with their mother. But when a mother is locked up, fewer than one in five stays with their father. The rest are sent to live with other family or are put into social care. Many have no contact with their mother at all. The imprisoned mother too often loses contact with her children and community. The system turns inmates into nomads.

One in three children with a parent in prison develops serious mental-health issues. Those children whose mothers are in prison are also more likely to follow in their footsteps and end up in prison themselves. It can be a vicious circle of crime and punishment.

Bluntly, locking up women is not the best way to reduce crime. The Scottish government's own statistics

One in three children with a parent in prison develops serious mental-health issues.

The imprisoned mother too often loses contact with her children and community. The system turns inmates into nomads.

show that women serving short prison sentences are much more likely to reoffend than those given a community sentence. Cornton Vale, Scotland's only women's prison, is the most violent prison in the country.

So how do we deal with women who commit crimes? Letting them go unpunished isn't an option. That would send entirely the wrong signal.

But SNP government ministers in Edinburgh don't have to look too far for a solution. All they need do is

dust down the report by the former lord advocate Dame Elish Angiolini. Two years ago the commission on female offending recommended closing Cornton Vale, and replacing it with a smaller jail for long-term and high-risk prisoners. When the findings of the Angiolini commission were published, the then SNP justice minister heralded them as a "compelling vision for the future".

Cornton Vale will soon close its doors, giving us a chance for a fresh start. It will be an opportunity

to move from custody to community-based sentences for low-level female offenders.

Yet the SNP government wants to repeat all the mistakes of the past by creating a new central super-prison for women at HMP Inverclyde. By pushing forward with this, the Scottish government seems determined to plan for failure. Instead we should focus on community-based sentences that would help to break the cycle of reoffending.

The Guardian, 18 January 2015
© Guardian News & Media 2015

MR BLUE SKY

Providing help to offenders through proper work

Prison doesn't work! Neither do cautions, court orders or fines if the objective is to stop people reoffending – people sentenced in this way have reoffending rates between 29% and 34% within a year. But prison works least well of all on this measure since 45% of all adults released from custody commit another offence within 12 months.

Almost 60% of those released from short prison sentences in the year to March 2013 went on to reoffend within the next 12 months: a total of 16,719 re-offenders committing 85,047 further offences. The National Audit Office has estimated that the cost to the economy of crime committed by offenders released from short prison sentences is around £7 billion to £10 billion a year.

It may be, as some would claim, that prison is too soft, prisoners are not punished enough, they don't learn their lesson. Or it may be that after a spell in prison it is not just cell doors that are closed but the opportunities that would allow a newly released prisoner to have a fresh start and earn a living without returning to their old ways.

Government plans

The government plans to change the system for the rehabilitation of adult prisoners in the community. 21 Community Rehabilitation Companies (CRCs), most of them combinations of charities and businesses, have a role in 'designing and delivering an innovative new service to rehabilitate offenders and help them turn their lives around'.

One organisation that can claim some success in doing just that is the social enterprise Blue Sky. It aims to rehabilitate offenders by winning contracts for jobs and supporting them while they rediscover their ability to work and with it their self-esteem.

Bank Robber & Banker

This is no set of inexperienced do-gooders. Deeply embedded in its working practice is the experience of one of Blue Sky's founders Steve Finn. Steve was a former bank robber who, unsurprisingly, had personal experience of how difficult it can be to find a job when you have a criminal record. He discussed the dilemma with Mick May, a former banker who was making a fresh start in charity work. Their meeting resulted in the founding of Blue Sky -

SOME ISSUES:

What is the purpose of sending criminals to prison?

Do you think prison prepares prisoners for life after their release?

What should be done to help rehabilitate prisoners?

> **Steve was a former bank robber who, unsurprisingly, had personal experience of how difficult it can be to find a job when you have a criminal record.**

a social enterprise with a difference - it only employs ex-offenders. By offering a proper job with a proper company, Blue Sky aims to break the cycle of re-offending and challenge ideas about ex-offenders. It also hopes to achieve real and long-term benefits for society. Steve, who was its first employee is now its Teams Director, managing all of the workers and maintaining high standards of work.

Employment

Not all the workers have serious criminal records but even a minor conviction can be a huge barrier to employment. The jobs are generally low-skilled as many ex-prisoners have no qualifications. This means that all training is on the job. It's important that the workers are engaged on productive work quickly both for their finances and for their experience of a regular routine which they must manage themselves. It also keeps them away from old colleagues and old habits. As Steve Finn told the Guardian, "When you have got a job for eight hours, that is eight hours when you are not up to something."

They are supported through a contract of up to six months and helped to gain further employment. The great advantage of Blue Sky, though, is that 50% of its full time staff themselves have a criminal record and have prospered by the

same process that they are guiding others through. The company also offers help with housing, insurance, education or even buying a car or van through interest-free loans.

Success

This all round support has won praise from those who have benefitted.

There's Mark who now has his own flooring business. Shanitta now works full time as a bus driver. She emerged from prison after a drugs conviction and proved to herself that she could take on the challenge of a job. Sharon had a conviction of actual bodily harm that arose out of a drink problem. She says of

Since its founding in 2005, Blue Sky has employed more than 1,000 ex-prisoners

A fashion show at the Old Bailey

Women in prison are a particularly vulnerable group.

Blue Sky's work programme "I want to prove that I can do this, I'm just so grateful that they gave me the chance".

Since its founding in 2005, Blue Sky has employed more than 1,000 ex-prisoners - that's about the capacity of one large prison such as Wormwood Scrubs. Only 15% of their employees have re-offended compared to that national average of 60% who reoffend within two years.

In 2012 Blue Sky began to work with and support prisoners within jails. The first Blue Sky Inside in-prison workshop was set up in Bronzefield, a women's high security prison in Middlesex. Female offenders are often an afterthought when provision or reform is made in the Criminal Justice System.

Women in prison

Women in prison are a particularly vulnerable group. 49% of women prisoners report having suffered from domestic abuse and 53% report having experienced emotional, physical or sexual abuse as a child. Women are generally on short sentences for non-violent offences but the effect on them and their families is severe. 49% of women prisoners suffer from anxiety and depression. Women account for 25.8% of all self-harm incidents though they are only 8.5% of the prison population.

Blue Sky's 'A Stitch in Time' is a textiles workshop which can employ up to 19 women. The workshop produces dustbags to protect the very expensive handbags for fashion label Anya Hindmarsh as well as jewellery bags for Scottish cashmere company Brora. In November 2013

49% of women prisoners report having suffered from domestic abuse and 53% report having experienced emotional, physical or sexual abuse as a child.

the workshop began a collaboration with fashion designer Sue Bonham which resulted in a charity fashion show at, ironically, the Old Bailey. Sue Bonham said, "Working with the women was an inspiring experience. Over a 12 week period the women, who thought they had little or no skill, discovered that with training they actually did have the ability to do some quite intricate work. It was a real pleasure to work with them and watch their progress."

Financial independence

One graduate of the workshop, Jo, used it to begin to prepare herself for a complete break with her past and a fresh start. Now relocated, with a new job, Jo explained, "It's great getting into a good working routine, having some responsibilities and being a role model to my children. I can be financially independent and can finally see a positive future. I feel like I am part of society again."

There is a strong push for governments to appear to be tough on crime. Prison numbers are climbing and, according to the Howard League for Penal Reform, three-quarters of men's prisons are operating above their capacity. The Howard League says: "overcrowded prisons lack the resources to house people safely, give them something to do and reduce reoffending following release."

Someone who leaves a difficult prison regime unqualified and with only a discharge grant of £46 (for people over 25) or £37 (for those between 18 and 24) must obviously be offered support if they are not to return to what they did before. Let's hope that the new Community Rehabilitation Companies will be as successful as Blue Sky in helping to reform those reoffenders who otherwise cost nearly £40,000 a year to keep in jail.

Sources: Various

Women are generally on short sentences for non-violent offences but the effect on them and their families is severe.

'CHED EVANS HAS SERVED HIS TIME' - AND OTHER COMMON MISCONCEPTIONS ABOUT THE CONVICTED RAPIST FOOTBALLER

A HANDY REBUTTAL GUIDE

LUCY HUNTER JOHNSON

SOME ISSUES:

Do you think that all crimes are forgiveable?

Do sentences reflect crimes?

Should criminals be able to return to their former life after committing a crime?

Should criminals be allowed to work in high profile positions?

Are footballers respected in our society?

Chedwyn "Ched" Evans, a Welsh footballer who played for Sheffield United was convicted in April 2012 of the rape of a 19-year-old woman, who was deemed too drunk to consent. He was sentenced to five years in prison and released on licence in October 2014.

After his release he was expected to resume training with his club but this opportunity was withdrawn in the face of a petition by 150,000 people, protests by celebrities associated with the club and, crucially, a decision by sponsors that they did not wish to be associated with a convicted rapist. Other clubs which considered signing Evans (including Oldham) faced similar protests and withdrew their offers.

Evans has not played professional football since his release. He has maintained that he was wrongfully convicted and his case is being reviewed by the Criminal Cases Review Commission - which can refer a case back to court if there seems to have been a miscarriage of justice.

Lucy Hunter Johnson offers a rebuttal to the argument that Evans should be allowed to resume life as it was before his conviction.

CHED HAS SERVED HIS TIME:

Well actually, he hasn't. Evans has been released under licence, but his sentence isn't finished yet, it's only the custodial aspect that is over. He could return to prison at any time if he breaches his probation conditions. He's not allowed to go abroad, for example. He is far from being a 'free man'.

HE DIDN'T EVEN DO IT:

A jury disagreed. The facts remain that on 30 May 2011, Evans got a text from his friend, Clayton McDonald, to say that he had "got a bird", neglecting to mention he had "got" her at 3am in the queue for pizza when she was so drunk that she fell over and twisted her ankle. In fact, she had drunk so much that she doesn't remember how she got to the hotel room where she eventually woke up, her clothes scattered around the floor. But this isn't about her

actions: it's about Evans. And he does remember. He remembers - and freely admits - that he got a taxi to the Premier Inn where McDonald had taken the 19 year-old, let himself into the room and watched his friend have sex with her. He then "got involved", while his brother and another friend watched through a window and tried to film it on their phones. Evans left later that morning via a fire escape.

Evans doesn't think this sequence of events makes him a rapist. But unfortunately for him the jury did, and it is from that foundation that all our conversations about Evans and his professional career should start. The Football Association are not able to overturn or ignore the decisions of our legal system. Should the decision be overturned in court, then it's a discussion that can be reopened.

Eamonn and James Clarke/Eamonn and James Clarke/EMPICS Entertainment

EVANS DOESN'T THINK THIS SEQUENCE OF EVENTS MAKES HIM A RAPIST. BUT UNFORTUNATELY FOR HIM THE JURY DID.

HE HAS BEEN PUNISHED, SO NOW HE SHOULD BE REHABILITATED

We need to be very clear what we mean by rehabilitation. Because rehabilitation does not mean a return to ordinary life, as if nothing has happened. Rehabilitation for Evans is not analogous with playing professional football. He could be rehabilitated without ever touching a ball again.

Rehabilitation is about reintegration into society, with the fundamental basis of this a reasonable understanding that the individual will not reoffend. And this is where we run into some problems, because Evans does not accept that he did anything wrong. In fact, he has repeatedly refused to accept even a modicum of guilt for anything other than cheating on his girlfriend. If he does not understand that what he did was rape, can we be sure he will not reoffend? He has shown no grasp of the issues surrounding consent, so can we really say he is rehabilitated?

BUT SAYING SORRY ISN'T PART OF HIS PUNISHMENT

No, but acceptance and a willingness to change is part of rehabilitation, which is surely the issue at question here.

SO ARE WE SAYING THAT HIS LIFE IS RUINED BECAUSE OF ONE MISTAKE?

Are we really suggesting that simply not being able to play professional football will destroy his life? The woman he attacked has just had to move and change her identity for the fifth time, after his supporters tracked her down and abused her. They even have a website vilifying her. Evans has yet to condemn their actions. Perhaps when talking about lives that have been ruined, we should first talk about his victim, and learn from his response to her ruined life.

IS HE NEVER ALLOWED TO WORK AGAIN?

Of course he is! But a rape conviction automatically excludes you from a vast number of professions. A convicted rapist couldn't be a teacher, doctor or police officer, for example. In fact, there can be few companies that would allow you to walk straight back into your job after leaving jail. Should football be so different?

BUT A FOOTBALLER ISN'T IN CHARGE OF CHILDREN OR VULNERABLE PEOPLE, HE IS NOT A THREAT. WHY SHOULDN'T HE BE ALLOWED TO PLAY?

Not a threat directly, no, but footballers are idolised, and - rightly or wrongly - presented as role models. Regardless of how he has acted since his release, allowing him to walk back on to a pitch to cheers makes a mockery of what he has done. Do we really want his face decorating the bedroom walls of young fans?

OTHER SPORTS STARS HAVE COMMITTED CRIMES IN THE PAST AND BEEN ALLOWED TO RETURN. WHY NOT EVANS?

A wrong decision in the past shouldn't stop the right thing being done now. This case should be judged on its own merits. And it is clear that public opinion now is overwhelmingly against Evans being allowed to return to professional football, with a petition to Oldham Athletic against the signing gaining 24,000 signatures so far, making it one of the fastest growing ever.

Perhaps it's because he has shown no remorse, or because he has taken no responsibility for the despicable actions of his fans, or maybe it's because he is so unwilling to learn from what he has done. But it could also be that public opinion is finally starting to recognise rape as the most appalling of crimes which deserves to be met with nothing but disgust and contempt for the rapist, rather than a new contract and football shirt.

The Independent, 5 January 2015
www.independent.co.uk

PUBLIC OPINION IS FINALLY STARTING TO RECOGNISE RAPE AS THE MOST APPALLING OF CRIMES

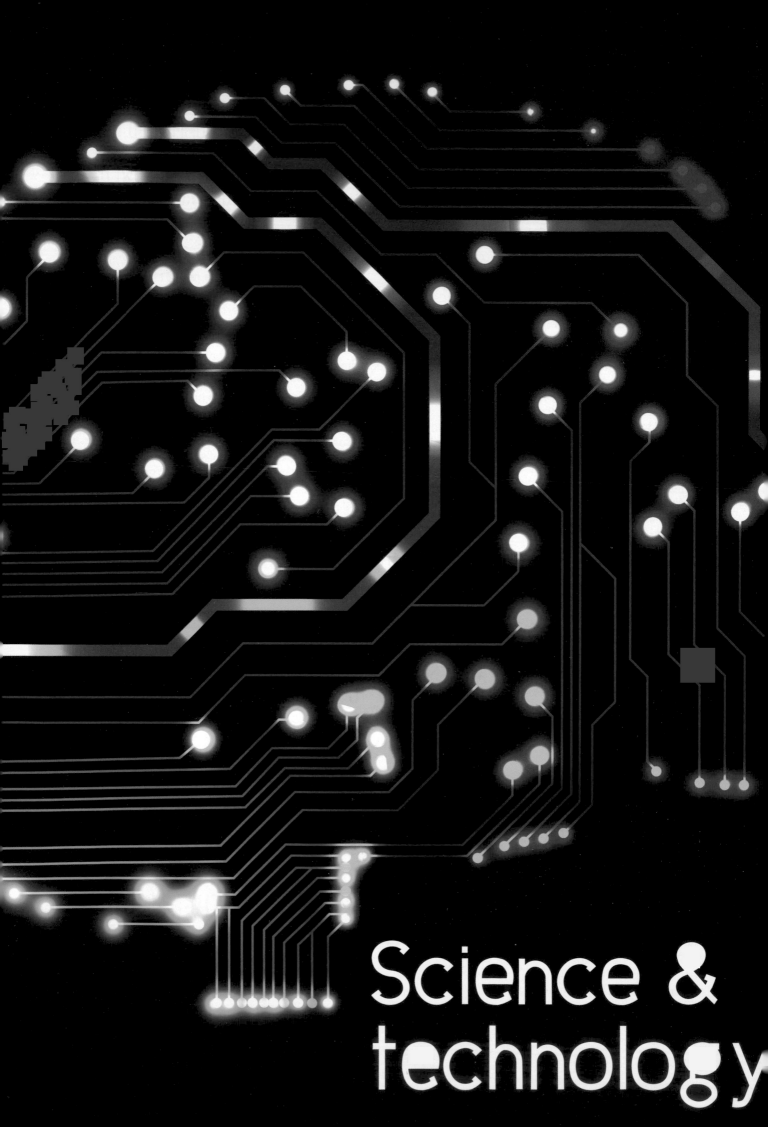

Science &
technology

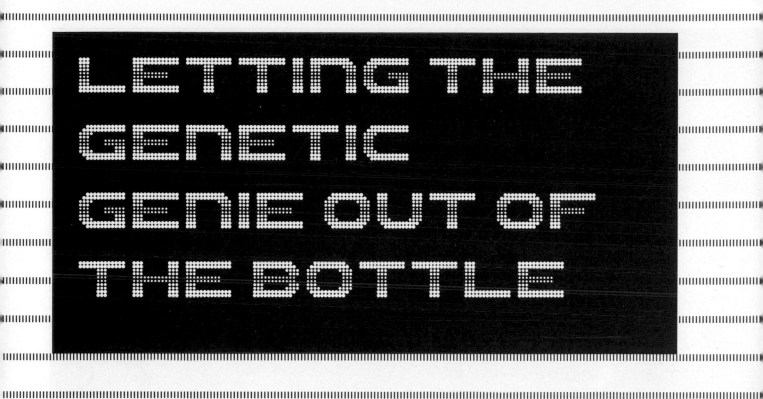

LETTING THE GENETIC GENIE OUT OF THE BOTTLE

Recent discussions of so-called "Three parent babies" prompt Mike Oliver to warn us to learn the lessons of history and guard against the relentless and potentially menacing march of science

SOME ISSUES:

Should we make changes to the genetics of a child if we can?

Does this type of action imply that all disabilities and conditions should be avoided?

What might be the negative effects of this type of intervention?

Do you think that these advances in science are positive or negative?

The UK is likely to become the first country to allow the creation of babies from three people. Following a free vote in the House of Commons and a relatively unchallenged passage through the House of Lords genetically engineered babies are now not just a future possibility but a current reality.

This recent decision seems to have been almost universally welcomed as an example of the ongoing march of scientific progress. Anyone who has questioned it has been dismissed as a religious fanatic or a member of the pro-life lobby. For the record I am neither.

Genetically engineered babies are a reality.

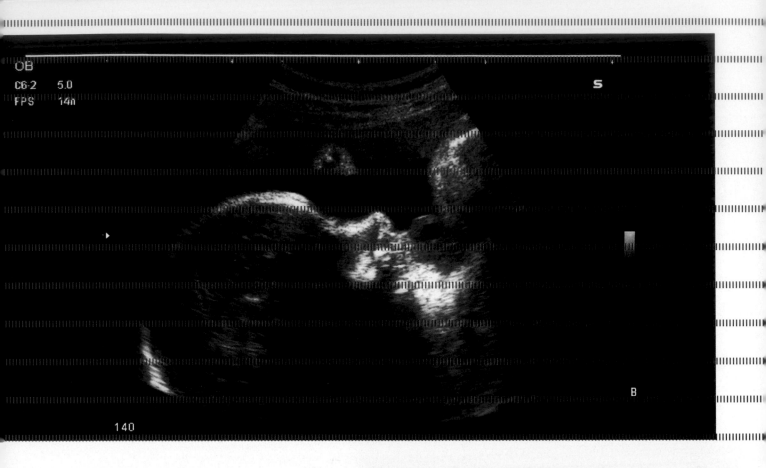

Even the heir to the throne, who has been remarkably vociferous about the dangers of genetically modified vegetables, has been ominously silent about the dangers of genetically modified people.

We shouldn't be too surprised about this as many prominent people in the twentieth century were also prominent in the Eugenics Society. One MP in the 1930s even proclaimed that it was necessary 'to stop the reproduction of those who are in every way a burden to their parents, a misery to themselves and a menace to the social life of the community'. While no-one would openly espouse such views today, the sentiment underlying the offensive language still exists.

The excesses of Nazi eugenics may have raised questions about where the science was leading us but the sentiment underpinning it remains alive and well today. While we may have challenged old stereotypes about us, many people still see us as burdens and tragic victims living miserable lives. These are dangerous times to be viewed like this as the global

WHAT IS THE ISSUE?

Some women have a known risk of passing on certain conditions to their children through their DNA. About 50 genetic problems can be passed on in this way, including diabetes, deafness, blindness and some heart and liver conditions, some of which are fatal during childhood. These defects cause serious illness in one in 6,500 babies, that's about 150 a year in the UK.

To avoid this, it is possible to use a special form of IVF. The nucleus from the egg which carries the defect is placed into an egg which doesn't. This hybrid egg is then fertilised.

Any child then born would have DNA from two eggs and one sperm - three parents.

382 MPs voted in favour and 128 against allowing this technique. Prime Minister David Cameron said: "We're not playing god here, we're just making sure that two parents who want a healthy baby can have one." Opposing him, Fiona Bruce, the MP for Congleton, countered: "[This] will be passed down generations, the implications of this simply cannot be predicted.

"But one thing is for sure, once this alteration has taken place, as someone has said, once the gene is out of the bottle, once these procedures that we're asked to authorise today go ahead, there will be no going back for society."

We must not assume that everyone wants to be cured

economy remains in recession and hate crimes are on the rise against us.

As disabled people we should be concerned and even alarmed about the lack of real debate on where genetic technology is leading us. As it becomes increasingly more sophisticated, we face the possibility that we will be able to eliminate more and more medical conditions and impairments. But who will decide which conditions and what will these decisions say about those people already living with these conditions?

When these questions have been raised, we have been told not to worry because potential parents will be given the choice about whether to make use of the technology or not. While this may be true for now, we have no way of knowing what pressures will be applied on prospective parents in the future.

Nor do the feelings of those currently living with impairments that can be eliminated in the future seem to have been considered. If genetic science is to continue it must take into account the effects it will have on the lives of those already living with such conditions and not assume that everyone wants to be cured or eradicated.

Already we have seen the withdrawal of benefits and services to some disabled people and their families and the rise of disability hate crime. Can we, in the future really guarantee the safety of those who didn't need to be born and can we be sure that the force of the law won't be used to prevent prospective parents from giving birth to impaired children? Recently we have seen leading politicians raising questions about whether benefits should be withdrawn from those with conditions that are seen as self-inflicted. Will parents who choose to have impaired children face this threat in the future?

But it is not just disabled people who should be concerned about the future but everyone, because the future of the human race is at stake. It is impossible to know who might be genetically engineered out of existence once the use of this genetic technology becomes routine. To give one current example; had it been available a hundred years ago Stephen Hawking might not exist so

there would have been no 'A Brief History Of Time' or 'The Theory Of Everything'.

There are many more similar examples and a quick tour through human history will show that many important scientists, engineers, artists, philosophers and the like were driven by a desire to overcome their own medical conditions and impairments. The effects of such engineering may well be unknowable but we can be sure that they will certainly harm rather than enhance the development of human culture and slow the rate of social progress.

Now I'm neither a religious fanatic nor a pro-lifer but I am concerned that the issues we are dealing with are more complex than they have been portrayed so far and that we should proceed with much more caution than we appear to be doing at present. We should be concerned not just for disabled people in particular but the human race in general.

Disability Now, 8 April 2015

We can be sure that they will certainly harm human culture and slow social progress.

Tom Solomon

The mystery of the incredible human brain

SOME ISSUES:

How important is it to spend time thinking about your brain?

How can we work at keeping our brains healthy?

Why do you think we fail to use the full potential of the human brain?

What else do you think the human brain might be capable of?

Throughout the day, different parts of your body clamour for attention: you get a rumbling in the stomach, and know it is time for lunch; you run too fast for the bus, and your pounding heart tells you to slow down and wait for the next one; you overdo it in the gym, and your muscles will let you know about it the next day.

But what about your brain? When was the last time you sat in a quiet, darkened room with no distractions and allowed your brain to think about itself? Maybe you never have.

Despite some remarkable advances, the brain remains largely a mystery. We know it is made up of about 100 billion nerve cells, called neurons, connected like wires in a giant telephone exchange. We know messages pass down them like electrical signals, and jump from one neuron to the next by release of neurotransmitter chemicals. We even know where many of the different brain functions, such as memory, sight, and smell, reside. But what we don't really have a grasp on is the link between the micro and the macro: how the pattern of electrical and chemical signals results in such amazing things as consciousness, intelligence, and creativity.

Much of our knowledge comes from studying brain function when things go wrong. One of the most famous cases was an American railroad worker Phineas Gage, who, more than 150 years ago, was cramming gunpowder into a rock with an iron bar when it exploded. The bar was fired up into his left cheek and out of the top of his head, landing like a javelin 25 yards away. Amazingly, Gage survived the injury, but he was not the same person; his personality had changed. Previously he was quiet and respectful, and had actually been the foreman. Afterwards, according to his doctor he was "fitful, irreverent, indulging at times in the grossest profanity… with the animal passion of a strong man." This loss of inhibitions releasing his animal passions was caused by damage to the frontal lobe of his brain.

150 years later, we still describe people as "frontal" if they are disinhibited by damage to this critical part of the brain. I have one such patient who always calls me darling, complimenting me on my gorgeous hair and blowing me a kiss. Although it is lovely to see her and she brightens up the clinic, this is not normal behaviour (especially considering the usual state of my hair).

Frontal lobe disinhibition is relatively common, but rarer brain conditions can give us even more intriguing insights. For example, I have one patient who was suddenly unable to read, even though his vision seemed normal. He could even write normally, but bizarrely couldn't read the words he had just written. This condition, known as alexia without agraphia, is caused by a tiny stroke, a blockage in blood supply, damaging the corpus callosum, a collection of neurons that connect the two halves of the brain. So although he could see the words and process the images in his visual cortex, his brain could not send this information to the language areas on the left side of the brain where it is interpreted and "read". Thankfully he improved over a few days.

During Brain Awareness Week, it might be a good time to stop and think about your brain, if you rarely do. The week celebrates an international campaign started in 1995 to raise awareness of the progress and benefits of brain research. Over the last twenty years there have been some remarkable developments. We have completely new drugs for inflammatory conditions like multiple sclerosis; we are better

The pattern of electrical and chemical signals results in such amazing things as consciousness, intelligence, and creativity.

at treating brain infections, such as meningitis and encephalitis; management of brain tumours and strokes has come on in leaps and bounds. But there are still enormous gaps. We have barely had an impact on the degenerative diseases, like motor neuron disease and dementia. In these conditions neurons just wither away and die, but we do not understand the basic triggers and disease mechanisms fully.

The death from dementia of the writer Terry Pratchett last week highlighted the huge remaining challenges in this area. He spent his last few years thinking a lot about his brain and its shrinking cortex. He even tried an experimental light treatment to slow the decay, but to no avail. Another author who spent time pondering his brain was Roald Dahl. He was fascinated by the impact of disease on this organ, believing that his own creative abilities were unleashed by a tremendous bash on the head in a plane crash. He also had the unique claim of helping develop a neurosurgical device - a valve to treat his son Theo's hydrocephalus, or water on the brain.

You may not have Pratchett's creative talents, or Dahl's inventive genius, but spend a little time this week alone with your brain. Let it know you cherish its extraordinary abilities. And if you are one of those people who attack it now and again with tobacco or excess alcohol, maybe for Brain Awareness Week just give it a break.

For Information about Tom Solomon's book on Roald Dahl and his fascination with medicine, see: www.liv.ac.uk/roalddahl

Prof Tom Solomon is Professor of Neurology at the Walton Centre NHS Foundation Trust, and Director of the Institute of Infection and Global Health, University of Liverpool. Follow him on twitter @ RunningMadProf

The Independent, 19 March 2015
www.independent.co.uk

Spend a little time with your brain. Let it know you cherish it.

Scientists are closing in on a cure for love, but should they go ahead with it?

Christopher Hooton

SOME ISSUES:

Can you think of any situations where removing emotions would be beneficial?

Ethically, what are the potential hazards to such science?

What else might this lead to?

Should science interfere with human emotions?

What are the pros and cons of this 'anti-love' drug?

At one point or another, all of us have probably felt like 'love', however we define it, is more trouble than it's worth. 'Love hurts' and 'heartache' are phrases most of us can relate to and a 'cure for love' was written about by Lucretius, Ovid and Shakespeare. But is love just a troublesome artifice we've created for ourselves, or a fundamental part of human existence, to be cherished even when it hurts us?

Advances in science might soon force us to face this question, as anti-love biotechnology would see feelings associated with love limited using medicine, with the concept being treated much like addiction or depression.

Neuro-ethicist Brian D. Earp thinks there's some truth to the old adage that 'love is a drug'.

"Recent brain studies show extensive parallels between the effects of certain addictive drugs and experiences of being in love," he told the New Scientist last year.

"Both activate the brain's reward system, can overwhelm us so that we forget about other things and can inspire withdrawal when they are no longer available. It seems it isn't just a cliché that love is like a drug: in terms of effects on the brain, they may be neurochemically equivalent."

Anti-love drugs are unofficially already in use, with Earp noting that in Israel some ultra-Orthodox Jews have prescribed antidepressants to young yeshiva students to reduce their libido, using the side effect of the drug as its main use.

Earp thinks there are certain situations where more sophisticated drug treatments could be beneficial.

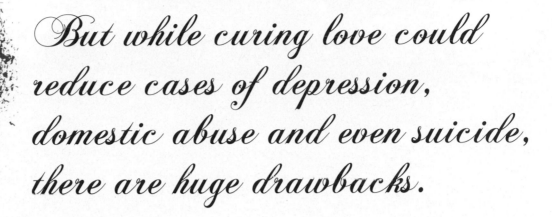

But while curing love could reduce cases of depression, domestic abuse and even suicide, there are huge drawbacks.

"You can imagine a situation in which a person's experience of love is so profoundly harmful, yet so irresistible, that it undermines their ability to think rationally for themselves," he added.

"Some people in dangerous relationships know they need to get out, and even want to, but are unable to break their emotional attachment. If, for example, a woman in an abusive relationship could access medication that would help her break ties with her abuser, then, assuming it was safe and effective, we think she could be justified in taking it."

"Even in a case of domestic abuse, that can be life-threatening, we wouldn't recommend forcing drug-based treatment on someone against their will: non-biochemical interventions should be tried first."

The dulling of extreme emotions and loosening of romantic bonds remain a side-effect of antidepressants that boost serotonin but in a digital age that makes relationships more

But while 'curing' love could theoretically reduce cases of depression, domestic abuse and even suicide, there are obviously huge ethical considerations and drawbacks.

Putting procreation aside, the treatment implies that heartbreak isn't a restorative learning process.

"It is important to be careful about making broad recommendations," Farp cautioned. "There are some people who are so devastated for such a long time after a break-up that they can't move on. Part of this might be depression, for which we already have many treatments.

intense and constant than ever, it's easy to see how they could become desirable.

In Japan, some men have already taken matters into their own hands. A social phenomenon known as 'Herbivore men' sees males shunning girlfriends or marriage to focus on their own lives.

The Independent, 10 February 2015
www.independent.co.uk

Sexual issues

DON'T TREAT YOUNG MEN LIKE SEX-CRAZED MONSTERS

Of course our children deserve proper relationship education. There's no evidence that internet porn is driving a wave of teenage violence - Ally Fogg

My oldest son, now approaching 12, is at the start of the difficult trip through adolescence. I have many friends with boys a little older, and meet other young men in my community. I simply do not recognise the dominant media narrative in the young men I know. They are not sex-crazed monsters, treating girls as meat before casting them aside and moving on to the next one.

What I do see is teenagers much as they ever were - gauche and gawky, awkward and insecure, hormonal, hyper and sulky. They are sometimes inspirationally brilliant and funny, sometimes stupid and self-destructive, and occasionally frighteningly aggressive.

I see young men desperately looking around and soaking up messages and cultural models for how to behave as a "real" man, many of which are downright

SOME ISSUES:

Do you think there is enough support and guidance for young people today, regarding sex and the internet?

How do you think the internet might be affecting people's ideas about themselves and life?

Why are boys more likely to turn to services like Childline than girls are?

I SEE TEENAGERS AS THEY ALWAYS WERE - AWKWARD, INSECURE, HORMONAL, HYPER AND SULKY

I SEE YOUNG MEN DESPERATELY LOOKING AROUND AND SOAKING UP MESSAGES AND CULTURAL MODELS FOR HOW TO BEHAVE AS 'REAL' MEN

Photo posed by model

toxic. It concerns me deeply that the political narrative that portrays young men as sexually aggressive, abusive and violent can easily become part of the problem. Young men who are at heart compassionate, gentle and kind cannot be well-supported by being constantly told they are the exceptions, when they are very much the rule.

There is no evidence that internet pornography is driving a wave of teenage violence and abuse, but it would be foolish to imagine that it is not influencing

sexual norms and expectations. Young people have to learn that in the real world not every sexual encounter lasts exactly 30 minutes, not everyone enjoys every sexual practice, most erections are not the size of a cucumber, and most plumbers don't arrive within 90 seconds of a call.

Boys and girls alike face a stressful journey through puberty and adolescence, and that includes navigating the risks of potentially violent or abusive partners. It is not an issue we can hide from or wish away, but nor is it the only issue. What has been missing from the recent debate is any sense that boys have their own issues requiring not just sympathy but attention, as an end in itself. They can be victims of exploitation and abuse. Young men have always worried about their sexual potency, prowess and attractiveness, their isolation and loneliness. Who is stopping to ask what impact ubiquitous internet porn is having on boys' own sexual insecurities and anxieties? Where do boys turn for emotional support, advice, guidance and reassurance? Certainly not to their mates, because the viciously policed norms of masculinity insist that we must never show weakness, vulnerability or fallibility.

In their advice to educators, the Sex Education Forum notes that boys have particular difficulties in admitting embarrassment or lack of knowledge, expertise and experience. They will often become disruptive and snigger rather than ask the questions they desperately want answered. And yet when surveyed, the same high proportion of boys and girls admit to being uninformed about crucial issues such as negotiating consent and happy relationships.

WHO IS STOPPING TO ASK WHAT IMPACT INTERNET PORN IS HAVING ON BOYS' OWN SEXUAL INSECURITIES AND ANXIETIES?

BOYS AND GIRLS ALIKE FACE A STRESSFUL JOURNEY THROUGH PUBERTY AND ADOLESCENCE

Teenage boys communicate almost entirely in braggadocio and bullshit. To do otherwise is to expose oneself to emasculating ridicule. It should be no surprise that a 2009 report by ChildLine noted that boys were more likely than girls to call about being sexually abused; nearly twice as likely to call asking about "the facts of life"; and six times as likely to call with worries about their sexuality. Where else can they turn when their schools are failing them?

Yes, children need proper sex and relationships education that acknowledges and reflects their world. Yes, let's teach children about enthusiastic consent, about mutual pleasure, about the true spectrum of sexualities and sexual pleasures in all their exciting, passionate, awkward, embarrassing, funny and often elusive glory. Let's start from the basis that all young people deserve empathy, support and education - not because they can cause pain and hurt, but because they can feel pain and hurt.

Twitter: @AllyFogg

The Guardian, 29 November 2014
© Guardian News & Media 2014

A version of this article first appeared on Malestrom, the blog of the Campaign Against Living Miserably

This is what sex education should look like

As someone who's experienced in this field, I know we need to teach children not just what consent is, but what it looks, feels and sounds like

Justin Hancock

SOME ISSUES:

Who do you think should be responsible for providing sex education?

Is the sex education you receive in school adequate?

Does it cover all the important things people need to know?

What sort of things do you think should be discussed in sex education?

Why is sex education important?

To many, offering lessons about sexual consent in schools sounds like a great idea. However, we need to go much further than just teaching "No means no" and "Yes means yes". Young people I work with know the definition of consent, but too often they have very little idea about what consent looks, feels and sounds like. Young people have usually not had a great deal of experience of this.

I've worked with many young people who I've had concerns about over the years. If I were to ask them whether sex they had was consensual, their immediate response would be: "Yeah, it wasn't rape." But if I ask them about whether they enjoyed it, how they communicated, what kind of sex they actually want and whether they actually want sex - then it can reveal a very different picture about just how consensual the sex was and how healthy the relationship really is.

It wasn't merely raising awareness about contraception that brought down teenage pregnancy rates, and likewise, we must do more than just teach consent in order that people have mutually pleasurable sex and relationships. We need to offer a comprehensive sex and relationships education programme for all ages. In particular older teens need to be offered something broad, challenging and inclusive - taught in an age-appropriate, evidence-based and confident manner.

To start with, we have to think about how we can both teach consent and give opportunities for young people to actually feel it. In my work with older teens, I invite people to shake hands with each other. By thinking about what they want from a handshake, and how they can ask for it, they experience consent and communication in a very real sense.

We often hear that young people are taught the mechanics of sex but not the emotional side of things. For the most part, I don't think we're that great at teaching either, and young people seem to agree. I think for many people in their mid-teens who are thinking of becoming sexually active, the only source of information about how to "have sex" is from the media (both sexually explicit and non-sexually explicit) or from actually having sex. Neither of which are ideal.

So we need to offer sex education that addresses

We can unpack what we mean by 'having sex' - that this is not just about intercourse or sex with a partner

this gap. We can unpack what we mean by "having sex" - that this is not just about intercourse or sex with a partner. We can teach that our bodies are diverse, and that people can enjoy different kinds of sexual activity at different times. Young people should aim for sex to be a mutually pleasurable experience for the first and every time, while understanding that not everyone wants sex.

Let's not lose sight of the fact that many young people also want to tackle the big issues around love and relationships. Why do people have romantic relationships?

Why should someone risk asking for what they want, when there is so much at stake? What does trust feel like? How can you have non-romantic relationships, and why they are valuable? What does loving ourselves mean? How can we act ethically in relationships? What are our values around sex and relationships?

If doing all of this sounds difficult, it's because it is. There are committed, experienced and well-trained teachers, youth workers and outreach workers out there who deliver excellent sex and relationships education - but there aren't enough of them.

Due to cuts many of them have left the area. Voluntary sector organisations are struggling to retain contracts and expertise. And those of us who have managed to stay in this field for a number of years have often faced attacks from the media and others. There are no quick fixes, and if sex and relationships education isn't done properly, it can do more harm than good.

The Guardian, 9 March 2015
© Guardian News & Media 2015

#THIS DOESN'T MEAN YES

In recent years there has been a change in public attitudes towards rape victims - a shift away from the suggestion that any woman is "asking for it" by the way she dresses or behaves.

Nevertheless, old attitudes sometimes crop up - implying that something the victim does or wears means consent to sex.

A campaign, promoted by Rape Crisis South London, uses real women to make it clear that clothes and behaviour cannot be regarded as consent - only a clear, willing and explicit agreement means "yes".

SOME ISSUES:

Why are campaigns like this needed?

Why do you think it is important to understand what consent means?

Is this a good way to highlight the issue?

What other ways would get the message across?

Perou is a world-famous photographer who specialises in fashion and portrait photography. On 11th April 2015, he took on a different role. On the streets of London, he photographed women, chosen at random, in a pop-up street studio. The photographs were composed in a way that felt authentic to the individuals.

The #THISDOESNTMEANYES campaign captured women dressed and behaving however they wanted, for no one but themselves.

This campaign says that 'this' – be it a short skirt, a low-cut top or a red lip - is not an invitation for a man to take what he chooses. It is a woman's personal form of expression, and her right to express it.

Photos courtesy of #thisdoesntmeanyes and photographer PEROU'.

A short skirt is not a yes
A red lip is not a yes
A wink is not a yes
A slow dance is not a yes
A walk home is not a yes
A drink back at mine is not a yes
A kiss on the sofa is not a yes

What I wear and how I behave is not an invitation

There's a myth that surrounds women, a myth that embroils them:
   women who dress or behave suggestively,
   women who are playful or who act provocatively,
   women who flirt or openly discuss sex
- they're 'asking for it'.

#THISDOESNTMEANYES #THISDOESNTMEANYES #THISDO

It's a dangerous and harmful fable, and it needs to stop.

every woman has a right to freedom of expression.

no woman deserves to be raped for it.

no one should be able to blame rape on a short skirt.

A short, skirt can't talk - a short skirt can't say 'yes'.

#THISDOESNTMEANYES #THISDOESNTMEANYES #THIS

Photos courtesy of #thisdoesntmeanyes and photographer PEROU'.

The only yes should be an active and embodied 'YES!'

This Doesn't Mean Yes is in conjunction with Rape Crisis South London. For further information go to:

www.rasasc.org.uk or call: 08088 802 9999

NTMEANYES #THISDOESNTMEANYES #THISDOESNTMEANY

War & conflict

The trial of Oskar Groening:

93-year-old Auschwitz guard admits he was 'morally complicit' in holocaust crimes

SOME ISSUES:

Why do you think young men like Oskar Groening found the military appealing?

Could Oskar Groening have done anything differently in his situation?

What sort of factors could lead to a party like the Nazis gaining popular support?

Could you imagine extreme political views becoming widely accepted in the UK?

Is anyone ever too old to face justice?

A frail, white-haired former Nazi SS guard has described in harrowing detail how he watched one of his comrades batter to death the baby of a Jewish prisoner at the Auschwitz extermination camp and admitted that was "morally complicit" in the crimes against humanity committed during the Holocaust.

93-year-old Oskar Groening, who served in the SS at Auschwitz from 1942 until 1944, shook visibly as he told a court in the German city of Lüneburg how, shortly after he arrived at the Nazi death camp, he was dispatched to the so-called "ramp" where prisoners were selected either for work or immediate death in the gas chambers.

"There was a little baby left lying behind on the ramp, after the main group was marched away,

and it was crying," Groening told the court, "I turned round and saw one of my comrades pick up the child. He grabbed it by the legs and smashed it again and again against the iron side of a truck until it was silent - when I saw that my world broke down," he added.

Groening, a weak and ageing widower, clad in a striped shirt and beige pullover, struggled into court with the help of a Zimmer frame and two orderlies. He faces charges of complicity in the murder of 300,000 Hungarian Jewish prisoners at Auschwitz during the summer of 1944. He is one of a handful of elderly former Auschwitz guards whom German justice authorities are hoping to prosecute before they die.

So far, however only Groening, who joined the SS as a

20-year-old during the opening stages of the Second World War, has been declared fit enough to stand trial. Legal experts have described him as "probably the last Auschwitz guard to face justice".

As his trial opened in a converted cinema in Lüneburg, Groening sat slumped in his court room seat opposite two elderly women, both Auschwitz inmates who managed to survive, and some 20 relatives of the estimated 1.1 million Jews murdered in the death camp. They stared at the former SS guard almost in disbelief. Several had flown from America and Canada to attend the trial.

Groening described himself to the presiding judge, Franz Kompisch, as an unwilling SS Auschwitz guard and claimed he knew nothing about what went on at the death camp before he arrived there in 1942. He said he had joined the SS as a young man because he wanted to be a member of a "smart elite" unit that "looked down on ordinary soldiers", explaining to the court: "They were covered in glory and I wanted to be one of them."

He said he realised things were different at Auschwitz shortly after he arrived because all the guards were given extra rations of vodka and sardines. "When we got drunk in the evening, the other guards told me that this was the place where the enemies of the German people were 'disposed of'. I didn't at first understand what they meant," he insisted. "Then I began to realise that Auschwitz was very different from the concentration camps in Germany."

Soon afterwards Groening was sent to the ramp at Auschwitz to sort out the belongings left by Jewish prisoners who were being sent to the gas chambers. "Then I saw what my comrade did with the baby," he told the court. "I

told him I thought what he did was wrong, but my comrade replied: 'What did you want me to do - run after the mother and give her back her baby? You can't do that. I had to kill the baby,' the guard told me."

The then 20-year-old SS guard said he experienced other horrors at Auschwitz first hand. "One day we were sent into some woods to catch prisoners who had escaped. Several were hiding in a barn. I watched as one of my comrades threw a gas canister into the building. I heard them all screaming. They were all killed. It was my first experience of gassing," he told the court.

Groening said he repeatedly asked his SS superiors to be transferred away from the death camp, but was refused permission until the last days of the war when he was sent to fight in the Ardennes. "Because of my job in Auschwitz, I am without question morally complicit in the killing of millions of people, most of whom were Jews. I ask them for forgiveness," he told the court. But he added: "Whether I am legally guilty is a matter this court must decide."

The former SS guard, who said he was weaned on anti-Semitic Nazi propaganda which depicted Jews as grasping, hooked-nosed "Enemies of the Reich" has been described as the "book-keeper of Auschwitz". A former saving bank employee, his job in at the death camp was to sort out the belongings and cash stripped from prisoners before they were sent to their deaths.

He maintains that he never injured a prisoner himself and insists that he has "never found inner peace" since the nightmare he experienced at Auschwitz. Holocaust survivors and their relatives have stressed that it is hugely important that a German court is putting Groening on trial. "Punishment is not the issue at

Despite more than 120,000 German investigations into Nazi war crimes after 1945, only 560 perpetrators were convicted by the German courts

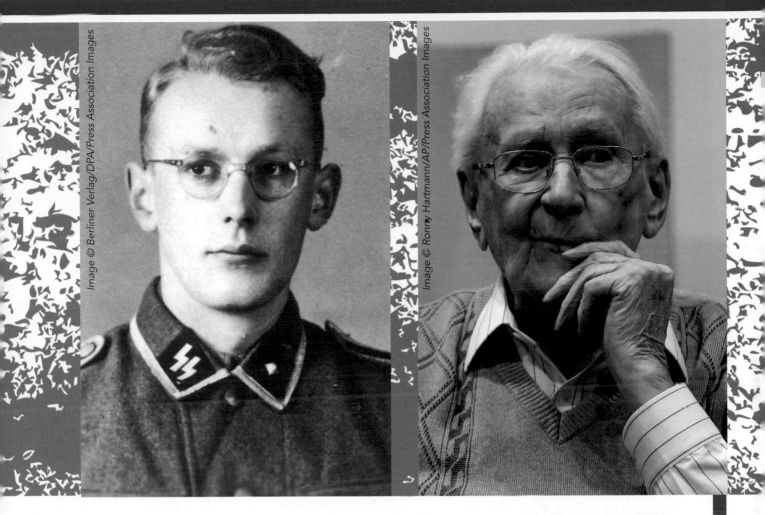

Image © Berliner Verlag/DPA/Press Association Images

Image © Ronny Hartmann/AP/Press Association Images

stake," 87-year-old Auschwitz survivor Hedy Bohm told The Independent. "We just want Groening convicted for what he did."

Despite more than 120,000 German investigations into Nazi war crimes after 1945, only 560 perpetrators were convicted by the German courts. Most were acquitted because judges insisted on the evidence of eyewitnesses in order to convict suspects. Thousands were let off because they claimed they were simply "obeying orders."

However the German justice authorities were obliged to rethink their stance following a legal precedent set by the conviction of the Ukrainian-born former death camp guard, John Demjanjuk, by a Munich court in 2012. Demjanjuk, who worked at the Sobibor camp in Nazi-occupied Poland, was convicted without witnesses, on the basis of his military pass

which showed that he worked at the camp. His mere presence at Sobibor, all of whose inmates were murdered, was enough to convict him of complicity in genocide.

Gabor Altmann, a Hungarian Jewish prisoner at Auschwitz lost his sister and her daughter on the ramp at the death camp after they were dispatched to the gas chambers. Gabor Altmann is, like Groening, now in his 90s. He now lives in New York but was too frail to attend the trial. But his daughter Sarah and her two teenaged daughters were in court in Lüneburg. "My father wants nothing more than to see Groening convicted," she told The Independent.

The Independent, 22 April 2015
www.independent.co.uk

Groening faces charges of complicity in the murder of 300,000 Hungarian Jewish prisoners at Auschwitz

On 15th July 2015, Groening was convicted of being an accessory to the murder of 300,000 people and sentenced to four years in prison.

A survivor's tale

How one woman managed to forgive the Nazis who murdered her family

Eva Kor, a survivor of the holocaust death camps, gave a testimony at the trial of 93 year old Oskar Groening. He was known as the 'bookkeeper of Auschwitz' because his role was to keep a tally of the possessions taken from Jewish men, women and children as they walked along the ramp that led to the gas chambers. To the surprise, and sometimes dismay, of other survivors she shook Groening's hand and did not shrink away when he kissed her cheek, signalling her forgiveness and her recognition that he was a fellow human being.

Betrayal?

For some survivors this felt like a betrayal. They felt that she had no right to offer such a public gesture and that it seemed to imply a disrespect for those who had died as well as a willingness to let those who had committed horrible crimes go unpunished. For others her gesture was an inspiration. A testimony to the power of human beings to overcome hate.

Forgiveness

For Kor herself, forgiveness was her salvation, something that brought her back to full life. She has often said that she refused to be a victim and her public gesture was part of a campaign to share what she had found, "I felt when I discovered forgiveness like I had found a cure for cancer. It was that amazing to me. If we consider anger and hatred the cancer of the human soul,

SOME ISSUES:

Why do you think forgiveness is considered a good thing?

Do you think there are any acts that are beyond forgiveness?

Can you understand Eva Kor's point of view regarding the Nazi party?

Can you understand why Eva Kor forgave Oskar Groening?

Appeal to your fellow Nazis

to make statements because, see, we the survivors – they don't believe us.

But you – this is your good job to make up for the bad job.

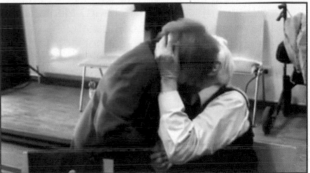

and if I found a cure for that cancer and it made me feel good and did not hurt anybody, should I keep it secret or should I share it with the rest of the world?"

She did not, however, deny that Groening had played a part in the Holocaust and that "he was a small screw in a big killing machine, and the machine cannot function without the small screws." But she felt that more good could be done by keeping this elderly man out of jail and using him to counter rising neo-Nazi groups and those who deny that the holocaust ever happened.

The testimony

To forgive is not the same as to forget. And Eva Kor had not forgotten the horrors she endured as can be seen in these extracts from her testimony at the trial:

"Hello Herr Oskar Groening,

My name is Eva Kor. In May 1944, when we were taken to Auschwitz, my name was Eva Mozes. My family and I were part of the Hungarian transport. My family included my father Alexander Mozes, 44 years old; my mother Jaffa Mozes, 38 years old; my older sister Edit, 14 years old; my middle sister Aliz, 12 years old; and my twin sister, Miriam, 10 years old. Within thirty minutes after arriving on the selection platform, Miriam and

I were ripped apart from our family forever. Only she and I survived, because we were used in experiments conducted by Dr. Josef Mengele.

Within half an hour we became part of a group of twin girls aged two to sixteen: thirteen sets of little girls and one mother. We were taken to a processing centre where they cut our hair short and took our clothes away. That evening they returned them with a red cross at the backs. Then they lined us up for tattooing.

When my turn came, I decided to cause them as much trouble as a ten-year-old could. Two Nazis and two women prisoners restrained me with all their force. They began by heating a needle. When the needle got hot, they dipped it into ink and burned into my left arm, dot by dot, the capital letter A-7063. Miriam became A-7064. Auschwitz was the only Nazi camp that tattooed its inmates.

Then we were taken to our barracks. They were filthy and crude. Huddled in our filthy bunk beds, crawling with lice and rats, we were starved for food, starved for human kindness, and starved for the love of the mothers and fathers we once had. We had no rights but we had a fierce determination to live one more day, to survive one more experiment."

Mr. Groening, tell the young neo-Nazis of today that the Nazi ideology created no winners. There were only losers.

Eva Kor went on to describe the experiments and how close she came to death.

"In Auschwitz, Mengele used approximately 1,500 sets of twins. The number of survivors is between 180 and 250 individuals. The other twins all died in the experiments. Would I have died, Miriam would have been killed with an injection to the heart. Mengele would have conducted the comparative autopsies. In normal life we cannot do that - inject one twin with a deadly germ and then perform an autopsy on the twin to see the results."

She recounted the story of how, before the liberation of the camps, the Nazis blew up the gas chambers in an attempt to destroy the evidence of their appalling brutality. She also explained that Miriam had been left with severe medical conditions as a result of the experiments and these eventually led to her death.

Forgive, not forget

Towards the end of her testimony she addressed Oskar Groening directly:

"My forgiveness does not absolve the perpetrators from taking responsibility for their actions, nor does it diminish my need and right to ask questions about what happened at Auschwitz.

I hope you will provide me with responses to the following questions:

1. How do you feel about my forgiving you and all the Nazis for what was done to us?

2. Do you know why Auschwitz was the only Nazi camp that tattooed its prisoners? Why did other camps choose not to do this?

3. Did you know Dr. Josef Mengele?

4. Did you hear about his experiments?

5. Were there any rumours about what Mengele did or what happened to his files?

Anyone who has heard or knows anything about our files, I still need to know what was injected into our bodies."

And she made this demand:

"Mr. Groening, I want to ask you to make this statement: "I want to appeal to the young neo-Nazis of today and tell them that Auschwitz did exist and that the Nazi ideology created no winners. There were only losers. Why create so much pain without any winners? It is sick to want to create another situation like Auschwitz. ..."

Eva Kor's full statement can be found on the website of the CANDLES Holocaust Museum and Education Center, which she founded. She has lectured extensively and in particular has three life lessons which she wants to share with young people facing difficulties:

"1. Never give up on yourself or your dreams. I did not know how to survive Auschwitz, but I was determined to do it. Here I am 70 years later because I never gave up.

2. Treat people with respect and fairness to eliminate prejudice from your life.

3. Forgive your worst enemy and forgive anybody who was ever hurt you. I forgave the Nazis and I forgave everybody who hurt me."

Her ultimate message of forgiveness is a survivor's message, her forgiveness is part of her resolution not to be a victim:

"I forgave the Nazis not because they deserve it but because I deserve it."

Source: www.candlesholocaustmuseum.org & others

"I forgave the Nazis not because they deserve it but because I deserve it."

GOETH
AMON
71- 0005
29 - 8 - 45

© Thorston Wulff

My Nazi grandfather would have murdered me

Jennifer Teege was sent to an orphanage at four weeks old and for 38 years knew little about her real family. Then, after a chance discovery in a library, she uncovered the horrifying truth . Etan Smallman reports

SOME ISSUES:

How much do you know about your ancestors - who they were and what they did?

Do you think crimes committed during war are any different from those committed during peacetime?

How would you feel if you made this discovery?

Jennifer Teege had been asking questions her entire life.

Born in 1970 to a German mother, after she had a brief affair with a Nigerian man, Teege was sent to an orphanage at just four weeks old. She had limited contact with her mother and grandmother, until being formally adopted by a couple at the age of seven.

Growing-up, Teege couldn't help but wonder about the biological family she'd lost contact with. There were so

many unanswered questions about them.

Then, seven years ago at the age of 38, the answers came in a terrifying deluge - along with a bombshell revelation about the grandmother she loved as a small child, and the grandfather she had never met.

Idly perusing the shelves of Hamburg central library, Teege happened across one of the collection's 350,000 books, a tome with a red cover.

Flicking through its pages, she realised with a start that a photo of a woman in a summer dress perfectly matched the picture she had of her grandmother, Ruth Irene. What's more, the photo of the author on the cover of the book - entitled I Have To Love My Father, Right? - look familiar, too. It was that of her birth mother, Monika.

"It was this immediate physical shock," she told me. "I felt this physical need to just lie down. I had to leave the library.

"I became weak because I knew that this book would give me so many answers. When you grow up with so many open questions in your head, this is something that turns your life upside down."

Her grandfather, Amon Goeth, had been a Nazi: the commandant of Plaszow concentration camp.

Teege was so startled to find any information about her family that the subject matter of the book almost passed her by completely.

It only hit her as her husband drove her home.

Her grandfather, Amon Goeth, had been a Nazi: the commandant of Plaszow concentration camp.

Teege recalls staying up all night researching his story online and feeling like she had "entered a chamber of horrors". She discovered that Goeth, called 'the Butcher of Plaszow' was "a man who killed people by the dozen and, what is more, enjoyed it".

He quickly rose through the Nazi ranks, slaughtering 2,000 Jews during the clearing of the Krakow Ghetto and up to 12,000 as the chief of Plaszow (a 200-acre camp built by the Nazis on top of a Jewish cemetery near Krakow, Poland).

What's more, he was a natural sadist. He trained his two dogs, a Great Dane and an Alsatian called Rolf and Ralf, to tear humans apart and would often ride around the camp on his white horse wearing white gloves and a white scarf. His costume was a sign to the prisoners that he was in a particularly vicious mood.

The Polish prosecutor at his trial in 1946, described him as: "a man who has become a legend in his lifetime for being the modern incarnation of the biblical Satan".

A man who killed people by the dozen and, what is more, enjoyed it.

Goeth's special brand of horror was given lasting infamy by Steven Spielberg in the film Schindler's List, with Ralph Fiennes playing the role.

His name has stuck in the public consciousness thanks to one scene in particular - where he takes potshots at prisoners from his bedroom balcony, described as "his personal form of morning exercise" in Teege's own book, My Grandfather Would Have Shot Me (an English translation of which has just been published in the UK to coincide with Yom HaShoah, the Jewish Holocaust remembrance day).

During that night of feverish internet searches, Teege, now 44, remembered having watched Schindler's List in Israel. She spent four years there as a student and learnt to speak fluent Hebrew.

And by another astonishing coincidence, or twist of fate - Teege is still undecided - in the course of her research, she discovered that her biological mother was appearing in a TV documentary about Goeth's death camp the following evening.

Teege desperately wanted to find an explanation for her grandfather's behaviour. She assumed - hoped, even - that she would find "some traumatic incident in his childhood that would explain his cruelty".

But Goeth's upbringing was perfectly normal.

Nor could she find any signs of remorse in either grandparent. Goeth's final act was a Nazi salute and shout of "Heil Hitler!" before he was hanged in 1946.

He quickly rose through the Nazi ranks, slaughtering thousands of Jews

Teege's grandmother, Ruth, lived happily in Goeth's camp villa as his loyal mistress, after the couple were introduced by Oskar Schindler. They never married but Ruth went to great efforts to take her fiance's surname after his death, a name Teege herself had until her adoption at the age of seven.

Right up until the end, when she committed suicide in 1983, Ruth had a picture of Goeth hanging above her bed. She used to gush about her lover as "a real gentleman". He had impeccable table manners, she remembered fondly.

According to one of Goeth's Jewish former maids: "Most of the time, [Ruth] was busy lying around with a cucumber mask on her face. She would turn the music way up so that she couldn't hear the shots."

Spielberg portrayed her burying her head in the pillow while Goeth was shooting from his balcony.

But it wasn't her grandfather's atrocities that shook her most.

Teege is keen to point out that, after the war, Ruth lived with an African and a gay man. "So she was open-minded. I have tried to analyse her. There's so much complexity that you can't define her."

Unsurprisingly, Teege was unable to leave the house for two weeks following her toxic discovery. She eventually sought help from a psychoanalyst who burst into tears during their first meeting.

But it wasn't her grandfather's atrocities that shook Teege most. Rather it was her grandmother's complicity.

The Nazi mistress was the person who "mattered most"

to Teege when she was a fearful and neglected child - who held her hand and "radiated kindness" until she was adopted.

"Her character is so interesting," Teege says. "She represents the majority of people during the war who followed the system.

"To differentiate yourself from my grandfather is very easy. Within my grandmother, it's easier to see oneself. It begs the question: How would I have behaved?"

Teege, a married mother of two who has established a successful career in advertising, has wrestled with the notion that she has Goeth's blood flowing through her veins.

She was disturbed by an article she read in 2010, detailing how Bettina Goering - the great-niece of Hitler's second-in-command - had been sterilised so she would "not pass on the blood of a monster".

Rather it was her grandmother's complicity

"I feel a bit sorry for her," says Teege haltingly. "This in my eyes is so fundamentally wrong. Because you can decide who you want to be, and to set a different example is better than to cut the blood line. Actually it was one of the quotes that inspired me to share my story with the public."

One also gets the sense that, with her book, she is trying to reach out to her mother. Monika agreed to meet her following the library discovery, but she has since

shunned her daughter's approaches.

Teege says with a smile: "I hope she has read it."

She also insists that the story will always have relevance:

"I hope that society has developed, but look what is happening now with Islamic State. I mean, there are people here from London - they grew up normally and they are following an ideology. There is still a danger out there that people follow blindly."

Writing the book, along with copious therapy, has helped Teege come to terms with her poisonous inheritance.

But it is also helping others.

"I met one survivor at my last event in Israel," she says. "He was in the front row and during the Q&A, his daughter told me that he was a survivor from Plaszow and his father was the personal shoemaker of my grandfather. He said my grandfather was his worst nightmare as a child and he wasn't sure at first whether he wanted to come to this event.

"In his words, he said, 'You are my birthday present'.

He was turning 80 the following week and he said he was really happy that he met me, because he could see that history does not have to repeat itself."

My Grandfather Would Have Shot Me, by Jennifer Teege and Nikola Sellmair, is published by Hodder & Stoughton

Daily Telegraph, 13 April 2015
© Telegraph Media Group Limited 2015

Using weather as a weapon!

Ian Sample, science editor, in San Jose

US expert Alan Robock raises concern over who would control climate-altering technologies if research is paid for by intelligence agencies

SOME ISSUES:

Who do you think usually pays for scientific research?

Where should the money for scientific research come from?

Does it matter what the research is for, and who pays for it?

Why might the CIA funding research be a problem?

How can we make sure research is only done for the good and benefit of the world?

A senior US scientist has expressed concern that the intelligence services are funding climate change research to learn if new technologies could be used as potential weapons.

Alan Robock, a climate scientist at Rutgers University in New Jersey, has called on secretive government agencies to be open about their interest in radical work that explores how to alter the world's climate.

Robock, who has contributed to reports for the intergovernmental panel on climate change (IPCC), uses computer models to study how stratospheric aerosols could cool the planet in the way massive volcanic eruptions do.

The $600,000 report was part-funded by the US intelligence services, but the CIA and other agencies had not fully explained their interest in the work

The use of the weather as a weapon was banned in 1978 ...

But he was worried about who would control such climate-altering technologies should they prove effective, he told the American Association for the Advancement of Science in San Jose.

Last week, the National Academy of Sciences published a two-volume report on different approaches to tackling climate change. One focused on means to remove carbon dioxide from the atmosphere, the other on ways to change clouds or the Earth's surface to make them reflect more sunlight out to space.

The report concluded that while small-scale research projects were needed, the technologies were so far from being ready that reducing carbon emissions remained the most viable approach to curbing the

in control," he said. Other funders included Nasa, the US Department of Energy, and the National Oceanic and Atmospheric Administration.

The CIA established the Center on Climate Change and National Security in 2009, a decision that drew fierce criticism from some Republicans who viewed it as a distraction from more pressing terrorist concerns. The centre was closed down in 2012, but the agency said it would continue to monitor the humanitarian consequences of climate change and the impact on US economic security, albeit not from a dedicated office.

Robock said he became suspicious about the intelligence agencies' involvement in climate change science after receiving a call

enough to change the climate, it would be visible with satellites and ground-based instruments. The use of the weather as a weapon was banned in 1978 under the Environmental Modification Convention (ENMOD).

Asked how he felt about the call, Robock said he was scared. "I'd learned of lots of other things the CIA had done that didn't follow the rules. I thought that wasn't how my tax money was spent," he said. The CIA did not respond to requests for comment over the weekend.

The US dabbled in weather modification before Enmod was introduced. In the early 1960s, researchers on Project Storm Fury seeded thunderstorms with various particles in the hope of diminishing their destructive power. A similar process was adopted during the Vietnam war, with clouds seeded over the Ho Chi Minh trail in a bid to make the major supply route for North Vietnamese foot soldiers too muddy to pass.

"I think this research should be out in the open and it has to be international so there won't be any question that this technology will be used for hostile purposes," Robock said.

The Guardian, 15 February 2015
© Guardian News & Media 2015

> "I'd learned of lots of other things the CIA had done that didn't follow the rules. I thought that wasn't how my tax money was spent"

worst extremes of climate change. A report by the Royal Society in 2009 made similar recommendations.

The $600,000 report was part-funded by the US intelligence services, but Robock said the CIA and other agencies had not fully explained their interest in the work.

"The CIA was a major funder of the National Academies report so that makes me really worried who is going to be

from two men who claimed to be CIA consultants three years ago. "They said: 'We are working for the CIA and we'd like to know if some other country was controlling our climate, would we be able to detect it?' I think they were also thinking in the back of their minds: 'If we wanted to control somebody else's climate could they detect it?'"

He replied that if a country wanted to create a stratospheric cloud large

> "This research should be out in the open and it has to be international so there won't be any question that this technology will be used for hostile purposes"

WOMEN ARE TO FIGHT ON THE FRONT LINE. NOW THE BATTLE REALLY BEGINS

Finally a change of Army policy will allow British women to serve on the front line. Emma Barnett explains what's really been driving the fear at the heart of this momentous decision - and asks what the future holds for our armed force

SOME ISSUES:

Why do you think the army has been resistant to allowing women on the front line so far?

Should the armed forces be different to other parts of society in terms of equal opportunities?

What attributes do you think are needed to make a good soldier?

"It felt totally natural - like I was supposed to be doing this. You know because at that moment it's you against them, right?" says Sergeant Brenda Hawke, a 17-year combat veteran in the Canadian infantry, when I ask how it felt to fire her gun at the enemy for the first time.

Having fought on the front line in Kosovo, Bosnia and most recently in Afghanistan, Sgt Hawke knows all too well about the grim reality at the coalface of war.

A year ago I travelled to Canada to meet women who have served on the front line. I wanted to try and understand why the UK remained in a rapidly shrinking club of countries who don't allow women into these close combat units.

My eye-opening trip, for a Radio 4 documentary, Women at War, was prompted by the news that our closest military ally, America, had finally changed its policy - leaving the UK as one of three NATO countries (the other two being Turkey and Slovakia - a rather odd group to be in) to prohibit women from serving in the infantry. At the other end of the spectrum is Canada, where these units have been open to female soldiers for the best part of two decades and (whisper it) its Army has been just fine. In fact it's even awarded medals to some of these women for their outstanding work and not special girly honours neither.

It seems the UK's top brass finally got the memo. A review into whether women should be

IN CANADA THESE UNITS HAVE BEEN OPEN TO FEMALE SOLDIERS FOR THE BEST PART OF TWO DECADES AND ITS ARMY HAS BEEN JUST FINE.

allowed to serve on the front line in the British military has been delivered to the Ministry of Defence after more than six months of research. Finally - the verdict is in. A change of Army policy will allow British women to fight on the front line.

It's the right result. Government officials had widely been expected to approve the change - after lots of positive murmurings from Philip Hammond, the then Defence Secretary (who described the armed forces as the last bastion of male chauvinism), when he commissioned it earlier this year.

Cue the many predictable howls of disgust - none more

pronounced than those of retired Colonel Richard Kemp, the former Commander of British forces in Afghanistan, who wrote in The Times last month, that women lacked the "ferocity, aggression and killer instinct" to be effective infantry soldiers.

Oh how quickly we forget, eh?

What about the 800,000 women who served in the Soviet Armed Forces in World War Two? Or the six thousand Russian women who joined the 'Battalions of Death' to fight in the trenches during the First World War? I hear the Kurdish Peshmerga's female soldiers are pretty handy with their weapons too.

Col. Kemp also trotted out the two other most overused and unproved reasons naysayers in these circles often resort to: allowing women on the front line will incur disproportionate cost and these lady soldiers will ruin the cohesion of these fighting platoons.

Understandably Brigadier Nicky Moffat, formally the Army's most senior female officer, is fatigued by these arguments, which she brilliantly describes to me as "sexism dressed up as concern".

"I spent 27 years in the Army and have heard all of these excuses before used to deny women roles. And yet, nearly all of the units which used to exclude women, such as the Royal Artillery Regiment, have one by one opened their doors. And women have proved themselves to be exceptional." Quite.

I would go further than Brig Moffat and say views like Col. Kemp's are not only wrong-headed but insulting to the military he is so proud of.

Thankfully, the Government agrees. With the lifting of this ban, our Army won't lower the standard of what's expected from these troops. Of course it won't. The same tests will apply and only those women and men who pass will make it in.

Valour - Canada's third-highest military honour).

Nor will ridiculous costs be incurred by allowing women into these units. Yes there will be some - for training and additional accommodation. But this is why our military leaders would do well to learn some valuable lessons from our allies across the pond in Canada - where separate sleeping quarters for different sexes on bases and missions were eventually axed - ironically because, you know, they needed to bond better.

Of course there will be teething issues. There were in Canada

that turned out. Rejecting somebody because of their sexuality, race and now gender, as opposed to raw skill, thankfully doesn't wash in most other walks of life anymore. Now, the Army has joined their ranks.

Now that the ban has been lifted, of course, we won't suddenly see women queuing around the block to join - not at first anyway. It will take time and only the best will qualify. But if our armed forces, despite being cut to the bone, want to continue to attract the brightest talent in Britain - it was vital they become proper meritocracies, in every area.

OUR ARMY WON'T LOWER THE STANDARD OF WHAT'S EXPECTED FROM THESE TROOPS. THE SAME TESTS WILL APPLY AND ONLY THOSE WOMEN AND MEN WHO PASS WILL MAKE IT IN.

Women, as they have proved in all other specialisms in our Armed Forces, do not degrade operational capability - they maintain it, alongside their male colleagues. No one, including Col. Kemp, would accept anything less.

Our Armed Forces' raison d'etre is to train individuals to the highest standards. No one is deployed into any situation they are not rigorously prepared for. That's exactly why Sgt Brenda Hawke could tell me it felt "natural" to pull the trigger to kill her enemy for the first time. Or why infantry Captain Ashley Collette had no issue with commanding a 40-strong all male platoon to attack with all their might, as they came under fire three times a day for two months during a particularly gruelling tour in Kandahar. (It's also worth noting that her outstanding leadership earned her the Medal of Military

and those other countries which have already taken the plunge. Sexism, harassment and in some cases rape, are all risks - but these ills sadly already exist in our armed forces. You can train a man or a woman how to shoot - but changing their 'banter' and mindset is a whole other battle entirely.

The last bastion of male chauvinism

No, the real elephant in the room is the culture change that will be required to transform the armed forces' very last all boys' club. That's what I believe is really bothering people like Col. Kemp. 'If it ain't broke why fix it?' is how the typical logic goes.

But these sort of lame 'justifications' were previously reserved for gay and black people and we all know how

Moreover if women are to ascend to the highest military rank, they cannot have any area off limits to them just on account of their sex.

Just be grateful

Having spent a few days with the new infantry hopefuls training in Canada, I haven't a clue why anyone would want to sign up. I winced watching their horrendous training schedule from the comfort of a bench, cup of tea in hand.

Instead of peddling tired myths about female soldiers' killer instincts, how about we try being very grateful to anyone, man or woman, willing to risk their lives on behalf of their country? Now there's a thought.

Daily Telegraph, 6 December 2014
© Telegraph Media Group Limited 2014

Brian Eno on the Israel-Gaza crisis: How can you justify this?

Brian Eno is a musician, composer, record producer, singer, and visual artist. He first came to fame with the band Roxy Music. He has been highly influential in the fields of electronic and experimental music. Eno is also a prominent anti-war activist

When the musician Brian Eno saw a picture of a Palestinian man carrying the remains of his dead son in a plastic bag, he was moved to write a cri de coeur to his American friends, asking them to explain their country's unconditional support for Israel. This is his letter...

Dear All of You,

I sense I'm breaking an unspoken rule with this letter, but I can't keep quiet any more.

Today I saw a picture of a weeping Palestinian man holding a plastic carrier bag of meat. It was his son. He'd been shredded (the hospital's word) by an Israeli missile attack – apparently using their fab new weapon, fléchette bombs. You probably know what those are – hundreds of small steel darts packed around explosive which tear the flesh off humans. The boy was Mohammed Khalaf al-Nawasra. He was four years old.

I suddenly found myself thinking that it could have been one of my kids in that bag, and that thought

SOME ISSUES:

What do you know about the war that Brian Eno is condemning?

Why do you think America is involved?

Who is responsible for making sure people know about what is really happening?

How much do people living in 'The West' care about what is happening elsewhere in the world?

Does this matter?

upset me more than anything has for a long time.

Then I read that the UN had said that Israel might be guilty of war crimes in Gaza, and they wanted to launch a commission into that. America won't sign up to it.

What is going on in America? I know from my own experience how slanted your news is, and how little you get to hear about the other side of this story. But – for Christ's sake! – it's not that hard to find out. Why does America continue its blind support of this one-sided exercise in ethnic cleansing? WHY? I just don't get it. I really hate to think it's just the power of Aipac [the American Israel Public Affairs Committee]... for if that's the case, then your government really is fundamentally corrupt. No, I don't think that's the reason... but I have no idea what it could be. The America I know and like is compassionate, broad-minded, creative, eclectic, tolerant and generous. You, my close American friends, symbolise those things for me. But which America is backing this horrible one-sided colonialist war? I can't work it out: I know you're not the only people like you, so how come all those voices aren't heard or registered? How come it isn't your spirit that most of the world now thinks of when it hears the word "America"? How bad does it look when the one country which more than any other grounds its identity in notions of Liberty and Democracy then

goes and puts its money exactly where its mouth isn't and supports a ragingly racist theocracy?

I was in Israel last year with Mary [a mutual friend]. Her sister works for UNRWA [the UN agency for Palestinian refugees] in Jerusalem. Showing us round were a Palestinian – Shadi, who is her sister's husband and a professional guide – and Oren Jacobovitch, an Israeli Jew, an ex-major from the IDF [Israel Defence Forces] who left the service under a cloud for refusing to beat up Palestinians. Between the two of them we got to see some harrowing things – Palestinian houses hemmed in by wire mesh and boards to prevent settlers throwing shit and piss and used sanitary towels at the inhabitants; Palestinian kids on their way to school being beaten

> I know how slanted your news is, and how little you hear about the other side of this story.

by Israeli kids with baseball bats to parental applause and laughter; a whole village evicted and living in caves while three settler families moved on to their land; an Israeli settlement on top of a hill diverting its sewage directly down on to Palestinian farmland below; The Wall; the checkpoints... and all the endless daily humiliations. I kept thinking, "Do Americans really condone this? Do they really think this is OK? Or do they just not know about it?"

> Why does America continue its blind support of this one-sided exercise in ethnic cleansing?

As for the Peace Process: Israel wants the Process but not the Peace. While "the process" is going on, the settlers continue grabbing land and building their settlements... and then when the Palestinians finally erupt with their pathetic fireworks they get hammered and shredded with state-of-the-art missiles and depleted uranium shells because Israel "has a right to defend itself" (whereas Palestine clearly doesn't). And the settler militias are always happy to lend a fist or rip up someone's olive grove while the army looks the other way. By the way, most of them are not ethnic Israelis – they're "right of return" Jews from Russia and Ukraine and Moravia and South Africa and Brooklyn who

came to Israel recently with the notion that they had an inviolable (God-given!) right to the land, and that "Arab" equates with "vermin" – straightforward old-school racism. That is the culture our taxes are defending. It's like sending money to the Klan.

But beyond this, what really troubles me is the bigger picture. Like it or not, in the eyes of most of the world, America represents "The West". So it is The West that is seen as supporting this war, despite all our high-handed talk about morality and democracy. I fear that all the civilisational achievements of The Enlightenment and Western Culture are being discredited – to the great glee of the mad Mullahs – by this flagrant hypocrisy. The war has no moral justification that I can see – but it doesn't even have any pragmatic value either. It doesn't make Kissingerian "Realpolitik" sense; it just makes us look bad.

I'm sorry to burden you all with this. I know you're busy and in varying degrees allergic to politics, but this is beyond politics. It's us squandering the civilisational capital that we've built over generations. None of the questions in this letter are rhetorical: I really don't get it and I wish that I did.

XXB

> "Do Americans really condone this? Or do they just not know about it?"

Wider world

Refugee children - fleeing from danger into danger

A young Syrian refugee carries his brother across the border between Greece and Macedonia, near Eidomeni, Greece
© UNHCR/Andrew McConnell

There has been a huge increase in the number of refugees seeking safety by moving within their own countries or to other countries. The United Nations High Commission for Refugees estimates that the number of people forced out had risen to a staggering 59.5 million by the end of 2014. This has increased from 51.2 million the previous year and is the biggest increase ever seen in a single year.

This means that one in every 122 humans is either a refugee, displaced within their own country or seeking asylum. The main reason for this increase has been the war in Syria. But conflicts in Afghanistan and Somalia, as well as other places, continue to force people out, as they have done for decades.

One of the very visible consequence of the conflicts, and the terrible suffering they cause, has been the dramatic growth in the numbers of refugees prepared to take dangerous sea journeys, such as those risking everything by crossing the Mediterranean.

What is not immediately obvious, but should be very alarming, is the fact that over half the world's refugees are children.

These children are fleeing from life-threatening perils such as recruitment as soldiers, child marriage and attacks on their schools. Often they are alone. Every year thousands of unaccompanied children make the journey across the Mediterranean without parents or other carers.

In 2014, over 10,500 children travelled alone to Italy by sea and over 6,100 asylum-seeking or migrant children were recorded as reaching Greece. 1,100 of these were registered as unaccompanied or travelling without family members. Actual numbers are almost certainly higher as many children travelling alone claim to be 18 or over so that they won't be kept in detention while places are found for them.

SOME ISSUES:

What should be done for children who cannot stay in their own countries?

Should all countries have an equal share of responsibility for refugees?

How could we put a stop to people profiting from these desperate refugees?

> **What desperation would drive people to risk everything - all their money, their lives - to travel to an unknown and unwelcoming destination?**

In May 2015, Human Rights Watch interviewed over 100 newly arrived asylum seekers and migrants, on the Greek islands. This included 41 children, most of whom were from Syria and Afghanistan. 24 of them, mostly boys between 15 and 17, were travelling without family members.

Some children said it had been their own idea to leave home but that their families supported them. The children or their families typically pay smugglers with money that they have saved or borrowed. Some said their families had sold their house to finance their journey.

Some Afghan refugees described walking 12 to 14 hours through the mountains in waist-deep snow to cross the Iran-Turkey border, and being fired upon by Iranian border police. Many said the most difficult part of their journey was crossing the Aegean Sea in overcrowded inflatable boats, arranged by smugglers who charged $800 to $2,000 per person.

What desperation would drive people to risk everything - all their money, their lives - to travel to an unknown and unwelcoming destination?

No schools means no future

According to Save the Children, at least 3,465 schools in Syria have been partially or completely destroyed since the war began in 2011. One Syrian man described how the government deliberately attacked schools where people were sheltering. His 10 year old son said that when his school was demolished, "I felt that my future was destroyed."

Tarek, a 16-year-old Afghan, said: "People are afraid to send their children [to school] because of the Taliban. One school is only open one day a week. Children do not go. The Taliban doesn't allow children to go to school. If families let children go, the Taliban will kill them because in the future they may work for foreigners."

Afghanis who fled to Iran found that they were discriminated against in education - which forced them to move on. Ahmad, a 16-year-old Afghan who was raised in Iran, said, "Two or three times I did well enough in exams to qualify for a special education program, but could not go, because I was Afghan.

Refugees are also not allowed to study in university in Iran, so I decided for my future to go somewhere else. I didn't want to go back to Afghanistan. Every day we heard about suicide bombings and someone or some group of people losing their life, even in Kabul. Every day there is a bomb blast. If I went back there, I imagine a dark future. I just want to have a chance to continue my education, nothing more."

Child soldiers - and worse

In Afghanistan, the Taliban and other armed groups recruit children as young as eight to serve as fighters and suicide bombers and to manufacture and plant explosive devices.

Akbar, a 17-year-old Afghan said, "I fled the Taliban, because many children who are my age are taken by the Taliban to use as suicide bombers."

In Syria, men must complete mandatory military service for 18 months, beginning at age 18. Hani, 17, said that the prospect of military service was the reason he left:

"I don't want to carry a weapon. I've never held a weapon and I won't do it. Not for the government, not for an armed group… I saw what was happening and I saw it would happen to me and decided to leave."

Child labour

Just surviving, for some children, was a desperate struggle.

Nasr, 16, began working on a construction site in Iran when he was 14, building walls with stone and cement. He worked 12 hours a day, seven days a week. He said, "If you took a day off, you would lose all your money."

Bakir, 16, began working in a garment factory at 14 with seven other Afghans. For his first year, he worked without a salary, from 8 a.m. to midnight every day, and during busy periods, even longer. The owner of the company told him, "If you won't work like this, you won't get paid."

Walid started working in Iran at age 9. He said he worked to enable his brother to stay in school. He first worked in a small garment shop, from 7am to 7pm, with only one day off each month. Later, he worked in a restaurant, but found that his wages were not enough to support him and his brother. "It wasn't a life," he said. "I was just alive."

Sayid, 18, fled violence in Syria at 16 and found a job in a Turkish factory. "It was long hours and little money," he said. "I worked from 8 in the morning to 7.30 at night. Sometimes they made us work until 11pm. We had no choice."

© UNHCR/Socrates Baltagiannis

A young Afghan boy and other new arrivals transiting through Turkey, disembark from a boat in the Greek island of Lesvos.

Firas, a 16-year-old from Aleppo, left Syria in early 2015 after authorities closed his school. He initially went to Turkey where he worked 12 hours a day in a garment factory: "I tried to save money, but other times I had to eat. I left Turkey a month ago. I couldn't handle much more work."

Child Marriage

An Afghan couple told Human Rights Watch that they fled Afghanistan to avoid child marriage. A 65-year-old man connected to the Taliban had proposed to marry their 10-year-old daughter. "If we didn't accept, they would kill us," said the mother. "He was connected to powerful people. I accepted the proposal because I had no choice, but I had a plan and we escaped in the night."

Safe - but in detention

Refugee children travelling alone are often detained much longer than adults or children travelling with their families, while the authorities search for shelter facilities for them. While adults may be released in just a few days, children may be held for three weeks or more. This is meant to be a protection for them, but many of them see it as punishment.

Asif, a 17-year old Afghan, said he had been told he would stay in the detention centre for three weeks.

"It feels like I'm in jail," he said. The children in the centre were not segregated from adults. "Last night, people entered my room and took everything," he said. "They say children should be protected, but it means nothing."

Leylo, a 16-year-old Somali girl who travelled for three months to reach Greece, had been in an overcrowded detention centre for nearly two weeks. She said that other detainees controlled access to the toilets, so that there were times she was unable to relieve herself. "They keep treating us like kids and saying you will go tomorrow, you will go tomorrow, but I don't see us going anywhere."

The life they leave behind, the journey and the destination all hold different risks for children who have few options and fewer opportunities. Jo Becker of the children's rights division at Human Rights Watch says, "Children forced to flee abuse or life-threatening danger and who encounter even more danger along the way shouldn't find more abuse and neglect when they arrive," Becker said. "Their own countries, the countries where they land, and other countries should be doing a lot more to protect and help them."

Source: Human Rights Watch
www.hrw.org

Image © Giorgio Savona / Demotix/
Demotix/Press Association Images

Farewell to America

For the past couple of years the summers, like hurricanes, have had names...

Not single names like Katrina or Floyd – but full names like Trayvon Martin or Michael Brown. Like hurricanes, their arrival was both predictable and predicted, and yet somehow, when they landed, the effect was still shocking.

Gary Younge

SOME ISSUES:

Why do you think there is such a big race problem in America?

Are things any different in the UK?

How should the police act to keep people safe?

In one incident, viewed widely on YouTube, a young girl was brutally treated by a policeman after a confrontation at a pool party. What effect is such an incident, and the publicity that followed, likely to have?

We do not yet know the name that will be attached to this particular season. He is still out there, playing Call of Duty, finding a way to feed his family or working to pay off his student loans. He (and it probably will be a he) has no idea that his days are numbered; and we have no idea what the number of those days will be.

But we do know, with gruesome certainty, that his number will come up - that one day he will be slain in cold blood by a policeman (once again it probably will be a man) who is supposed to protect him and his community. We know this because it is statistically inevitable and has historical precedent. We know this because we have seen it happen again and again. We know this because this is not just how America works; it is how America was built. Like a hurricane, we know it is coming - we just do not yet know where or when or how much damage it will do.

Image © Rena Schild / Shutterstock.com

This is the summer I will leave America, after 12 years as a foreign correspondent, and return to London. My decision to come back to Britain was prompted by banal, personal factors that have nothing to do with current events; if my aim was to escape aggressive policing and racial disadvantage, I would not be heading to Hackney.

But while the events of the last few years did not prompt the decision to come back, they do make me relieved that the decision had already been made. It is why I have not once had second thoughts. If I had to pick a summer to leave, this would be the one. Another season of black parents grieving, police chiefs explaining. Another season when America has to be reminded

that black lives matter because black deaths at the hands of the state have been accepted as routine for so long. A summer ripe for rage.

I arrived in New York just a few months before the Iraq war. Americans seemed either angry at the rest of the world, angry at each other, or both.

I saw it as my mission to try and understand the US.

On the weekend in 2007 that Barack Obama declared his presidential candidacy, our son was born. Six years later, we had a daughter. For the most part I have kept my English accent. But my language relating to children is reflexively American: diapers, strollers, pacifiers, recess, candy and long pants. I have only ever been a parent here - a role for which my own upbringing in England provides no real reference point.

The day we brought my son home, an article in the New York Times pointed out that in America "a black male who drops out of high school is 60 times more likely to find himself in prison than one with a bachelor's degree". Previously, I'd have found that interesting and troubling. Now it was personal. I had skin in the game. Black skin in a game where the odds are stacked against it.

The symbolic advantages of Obama's election were clear. For two years I pushed my son around in his stroller surrounded by a picture of a black man framed by the

My son was with a four-year-old white friend who looked up from his Thomas the Tank Engine and told my son: "You're black."

words "Hope" and "Change". A year or so after Obama came to office, my son had a playdate with a four-year-old white friend who looked up from his Thomas the Tank Engine and told my son: "You're black." It was a reasonable thing for a child of that age to point out - he was noticing difference, not race. But when my son looked at me for a cue, I now had a new arrow in my quiver to deflect any potential awkwardness. "That's right," I said. "Just like the president."

But the substantial benefits were elusive. Obama inherited an economic crisis that hurt African Americans more than any other community. The discrepancy between black and white employment and wealth grew during his first few years and has barely narrowed since.

Class does makes a big difference, of course: this is America. We [my family] have healthcare, jobs, university educations and a car; we live in a community with reasonable schools, supermarkets and restaurants. In short, we have resources and therefore we have options.

We do not, however, have the option not to be black. And in this time and this place that is no minor factor. Class offers a range of privileges; but it is not a sealant that protects you from everything else.

We would have to live in an area with few other black people, since black neighbourhoods are policed with insufficient respect for life or liberty; send our children to a school with few other black students, since majority-black schools are underfunded; tell them not to wear anything that would associate them with black culture, since doing so would make them more vulnerable to profiling; tell them not to mix with other black children, since they are likely to live in the very areas and go to the very schools from which we would be trying to escape; and not let the children go out after dark, since being young and black after sunset makes the police suspect that you have done or are about to do something.

The list could go on. None of this self-loathing behaviour would provide any guarantees, of course.

Trayvon Martin* was walking through a gated community when George Zimmerman pegged him for a thug and shot him dead. Clementa Pinckney*, a South Carolina state senator, was in one of Charleston's most impressive churches when Dylann Roof murdered him and eight others.

I have not only never met an African American who thought they could buy themselves the advantages of a white American; I have yet to meet one who thinks they can even buy themselves out of the disadvantages of being black. All you can do is limit the odds. And when one in three black boys born in 2001 is destined for the prison system, those odds are pretty bad. Having a black man in the White House has not changed that.

Most days, the park closest to us looks like Sesame Street. White, black and Vietnamese American kids climbing, swinging and sliding. Occasionally, particularly late on weekday afternoons, teenagers show up. Like adolescents the western world over, they are bored, broke, horny and lost. They don't want to stay at home, but can't afford to be anywhere that costs money, and so they come to the public space most approximate to their needs, where they squeeze into swings that are meant for smaller kids and joke, flirt and banter. Very occasionally they swear and get a little rowdy - but nothing that an adult could not deal with by simply asking them to keep the language down because there are little kids around. Oh, and in

* TRAYVON MARTIN: 26 February, 2012, in Florida, there was an altercation between George Zimmerman a 28-year-old mixed-race Hispanic man who was a neighbourhood watch volunteer and Trayvon Martin, a 17-year-old African American high school student. Zimmerman shot Martin, who was unarmed. He claimed to havie acted in self-defence, and on 1 July, 2013, a jury acquitted him of second-degree murder.

* CLEMENTA PINCKNEY: On 17 June, 2015, Dylann Roof, a 21 year old white man entered a church in Charleston, South Carolina where an evening of Bible study was in progress and shot dead nine black people including the minister, Clementa Pinckney, who was also a state Senator. The shooting was apparently motivated by racial hatred as Roof had posted white supremacist messages on his Facebook page.

this park the teenagers are usually black.

Their presence certainly changes the mood. But the only time it ever really gets tense is when the police come. The better police chat with them, the worse ones interrogate them. Either way, the presence of armed, uniformed people in this children's space is both unsettling and unnecessary.

Once, when some adolescents were hanging out relatively quietly one afternoon, I struck up a conversation with a white woman. Her son was roughly the same age as mine, we both lived nearby and neither of our kids would have to cross a road to get to the park. We were discussing at what age we thought it would be appropriate to let our boys come by themselves. "The thing is, you just don't know if it's going to be quiet or if the junior gangbangers are going to be hanging around," she said, gesturing to the youths on the swings.

This woman and I were looking at the same kids but seeing quite different things.

When George Zimmerman saw Trayvon Martin, he didn't see a 17-year-old boy walking home from the store. He saw someone "real suspicious", "up to no good", whom he assumed bore some responsibility for recent burglaries.

Last summer, on the afternoon I arrived home from reporting on the disturbances after Michael Brown's* death in Ferguson, Missouri,

Image © Rena Schild / Shutterstock.com

there was a barbecue and music at the local park. I took the kids. The park has a water feature that shoots wet jets from the ground and sprays kids in fountains from all sides as they paddle around. The younger ones peel down to their underwear while the older ones just pile in whatever they have on. It was a scorching day and my son and several other kids were having a water fight - a tame affair with very little collateral damage for those not involved beyond the odd sprinkling. At one stage, while in hot pursuit of his main rival, my son splashed a woman on her leg. She yelled at him as though he'd hit her with a brick.

I'd seen the whole thing and ran over.
"What's the problem?" I said.
"Look. He's covered me in water," she shouted.
I looked. She was barely wet. But even if he had...
"You're standing in a children's park, on a hot day, next to a

> This woman and I were looking at the same kids but seeing quite different things.

water feature," I said. "Deal with it. Just stop shouting at him."

"Don't you tell me what to do," she barked.

"Now you're shouting at me," I said. "Just stop it."

"Who the hell are you?" she yelled.

"I'm his dad that's who."

"You're nobody, that's who you are," she bellowed. "Nobody."

Raising a black child in a racist society poses a very particular set of challenges. On the one hand, you want them to be proud and confident of who they are. On the other, you have to teach them that they are vulnerable precisely because of who they are, in the knowledge that awareness of that vulnerability just might save their life.

While I have been in America, I have not been shot at, arrested, imprisoned or otherwise seriously inconvenienced by the state. I do not live in the hollowed out, jobless zones of urban economic despair to which many African Americans have been abandoned. I have been shouted at in a park, taken different routes to school, and occasionally dealt with bigoted officials. (While driving through Mississippi to cover Katrina I approached a roadblock that all the other journalists had easily passed through, only to have a policeman pat the gun in his holster and turn me around). These experiences are aggravating. They are not life-threatening.

I am not Michael Brown. But then Michael Brown wasn't Michael Brown before he was shot dead and had his body left on the street for four hours; *Eric Garner was just a man trying to sell cigarettes in the street before he was choked to death in Staten Island; *Tamir Rice was just a boisterous kid acting out in a park before a policeman leaped out of his squad car and shot him within seconds. Being shot dead by the police or anyone else is not the daily experience of black people in America.

It is exhausting. When the videos of brutality go viral I can't watch them unless I have to write about them. I don't need to be shocked - which is just as well because these videos emerge with such regularity that they cease to be shocking.

*MICHAEL BROWN: On 9 August, 2014, Michael Brown had been involved in a small scale robbery at a convenience store. He was stopped on the street by a white police officer, Darren Wilson. The pair struggled, with Brown reaching through the window of the police car. He then ran away and the officer ran after him. When Brown, who was unarmed, turned to face him the officer shot him several times, the last bullet killed him.

The shooting provoked civil unrest in the town of Ferguson and beyond. In 2015 the US Department of Justice found that the policeman had acted in self defence.

*ERIC GARNER: On 17 July, 2014, in Staten Island, New York City, Eric Garner was approached by police who accused him of selling loose, single cigarettes. In an altercation, Garner was pulled to the ground by an officer who put his arm round his neck and he was then pinned face down by four officers. He was heard to say repeatedly "I can't breathe". When he lost consciousness he was turned on his side to await an ambulance. He was pronounced dead on arrival at hospital.

A grand jury decided not to prosecute the officer who had put a hold on Garner for about 15 seconds. Protesters used "I can't breathe" as a slogan and a hashtag.

*TAMIR RICE: On 22 November, 2014, in Cleveland Ohio, a caller reported to the police that there was a male black in a city park sitting on a swing and pointing a gun at people. The caller also said "it's probably fake" and "he's probably a juvenile".

One of the two policemen who responded fired two shots at 12 year old Tamir Rice within two seconds of arriving and from a distance of only ten feet. Tamir was holding a toy gun from which someone had removed the orange safety markings. One bullet hit him in the torso causing major injury. Neither officer gave first aid and the boy died the next day.

At the time of writing it is not clear whether anyone will be charged over this incident.

The altercations in the park, the rerouted walks to school, the aggravations of daily life are the lower end of a continuum - a dull drumbeat that occasionally crescendos into violent confrontation and even social conflagration.

Seven children and teenagers are shot on an average day in the US. I have just finished writing a book in which I take a random day and interview the families and friends of those who perished. Ten young people died the day I chose. Eight were black. All of the black parents said they had assumed this could happen to their son.

As one bereaved dad told me: "You wouldn't be doing your job as a father if you didn't."

The Guardian, 1 July 2015
© Guardian News & Media 2015

One of the two policemen who responded fired two shots at 12 year old Tamir Rice within two seconds of arriving and from a distance of only ten feet.

Tamir was holding a toy gun.

Image © Bryan Sutter / Demotix/Demotix/Press Association Images

Unusual arrangements

We are familiar with 'arranged marriages' but two personal ads show how society in India is starting to change.

Marriages all over the world share some common features. There's emotion of course - the bond between the bride and groom, not to mention the tensions that often surface at weddings. There's family, the existing ones that you need to accommodate and appease and the new ones that you must learn to accept. There are traditions and social obligations. And then, of course, there's the cost.

For families from the Indian sub-continent marriage means all of the above to the power of ten. The families are bigger, the traditions more powerful and the costs sometimes ruinously high.

There's a big investment in marriage, a great deal of shame in divorce, and a strong compulsion to get it right. Matchmaking is therefore critically important and arranged marriages - with varying degrees of choice - are still common both in the sub-continent and within Asian communities in the west. Marriages are made not in heaven but increasingly in small ads and websites where interests and expectations are laid out in some detail.

Ads are often posted by the family, as in this example from a matchmaking website:

"My daughter is a well educated, professionally qualified and beautiful girl. She is brought up with Indian traditional family values with modern outlook. Loves to travel, watch movies and is an amazing cook. We are a close knit family and I have 4 daughters. She is the 3rd eldest. Her 2 elder sisters are married and well settled."

And another about a son: *"He is an optimistic, down-to-earth, presentable and an understanding person with pleasing personality. People noticed him as somebody who is level-headed, matured, humble and family-oriented."*

But things might be changing if two recent examples are anything to go by.

When Indhuja Pillai saw that her parents had put her profile on a matrimony site she was astonished. Not only did she not want it posted, it sounded nothing like her. It was more like the traditional description found throughout these websites and, as she says herself, Indhuja is "no ordinary (read: mainstream) woman desperate to get married".

She took matters into her own hands and wrote her own profile - one that was unlike any other- and placed it on her own website - marry.indhuja.com.

She told her parents, "Send this to anyone who has the nerve to ask for my hand in marriage."

While the basic information is relatively conventional - though she describes her gender as 'tomboy' and her status as 'married to self' - it is when Indhuja describes what she wants, and doesn't want in a husband, that she really sets herself apart:

"More info - I'm not a drinker and I hate smoking. An eggitarian, not a foodie. I play badminton, sing and dance. I wear glasses and look dorky in them. Not a spendthrift or a shopaholic. Detest masala & drama, not a TV fan. I don't read. Friendly but I don't prefer friendship. NOT a womanly woman. Definitely not marriage material. Won't grow long hair, ever. I come with a life-long guarantee and I commit for life.

Looking for: A man, preferably bearded, who is passionate about seeing the world. Someone who earns for himself and does NOT hate his job. Must be flexible

SOME ISSUES:

Do you think traditions are a positive or negative thing?

Should parents be involved in deciding who their child marries?

Do these adverts seem progressive in Indian culture?

If you had to write an advert for yourself what would it say?

with his parents, also means, it's better if he is NOT a family guy. Extra points to the one who hates kids. Points for a great voice and an impressive personality. Should be able to hold a conversation for at least 30 minutes."

And if that is not a sufficient deterrent she adds:
"If you think you qualify, I recommend you re-think. If you are sure, I suggest you show this website to your parents. If you're still sure, try imagining a life with someone like me.

Unsure? click the 'X' and get back to what you were doing. Sure? Drop me a message on Facebook or tweet to me."

Her website was an immediate success. She was contacted by many men and women, who themselves felt obliged to fit in with their parents expectations and conventions, and who praised her for her honesty. She says "Many women could relate to the plight of their parents pestering them to get married. And men, without a choice, could only dream of marrying someone like the woman in the profile, me."

Seemingly more traditional, actually more radical in Indian society is this matrimonial advert which appeared in May 2015:

"Seeking 25-40, Well Placed, Animal-Loving, Vegetarian Groom for my son (36, 5'11")"

The advert was placed in the traditional way, by the mother of Harish Iyer, an Indian gay rights activist, who says, "My mother is like any other mother. She wanted to find me a partner and help me settle down. It became news only because I was looking for a man instead of a woman."

Until recently this would have been an unusual act in many countries. In India it is a particularly brave and controversial one since homosexuality was made a criminal act once more in 2013.

The ad was refused by several newspapers on the grounds that it was illegal but was published by the daily newspaper Mid-Day.

Mr Iyer says of his mother "She is going through the proposals, she will draw a shortlist and tell me who to meet. I am looking forward to meet them. I am hoping to find a partner now."

While there is a movement in India demanding equal rights, there is also strong religious and political opposition to any liberalisation and Mr Iyer is unlikely ever to be able to marry.

This being so, the advert was undoubtedly not a serious plea for a partner but rather a piece of activism, designed to draw publicity, and highlight inequality. However, one part of his mother's advert harks back to a conservative, traditional, Indian marriage arrangement and strikes a sour note as part of a campaign for equality. The advert says "Caste no bar" - but it also says "Although Iyer preferred" - a reference to the upper class Brahmin community and therefore to the caste system which has been responsible for many injustices within society.

It seems particularly difficult to escape some aspects of a traditional Indian marriage - family, money and status all matter. But possibly these adverts, and the responses they are getting, hint that some people are ready for change.

Sources: Various

The advert was undoubtedly not a serious plea for a partner

The right to offend?

On 7 January 2015 two gunmen forced their way into the Paris headquarters of the satirical magazine, Charlie Hebdo, killing twelve people and wounding eleven. The gunmen were two French brothers, whose family originally came from Algeria, and whose motivation became clear in their cries of "the Prophet is avenged".

Charlie Hebdo regularly and routinely satirised and mocked authority, heads of state and all global religions. This magazine, with a tiny circulation, had been targeted, just as it had been fire-bombed in 2011, because it published cartoons of the prophet Muhammad amongst its other religious and political subjects. The gunmen killed editors and cartoonists as well as a guest, a caretaker and police in what the French Prime Minister described as a "terrorist attack of the most extreme barbarity".

A shocked world responded with demonstrations of support - both symbolic and practical. The hashtag #JeSuisCharlie appeared on posters, badges and websites, it replaced profile pictures on Facebook. The survivors of the attack announced the next day that they would publish an edition of the paper and the print run had to be increased from the usual 60,000 to 8 million in order to meet the demand. The money from this and from donations from media groups was to go to the families of the victims. Suddenly a small-circulation, satirical magazine was headline news and shorthand for the defence of free speech.

On the Sunday following the attack, a huge protest march was held in Paris, with matching protests in many cities. Ironically the Paris march was led (with a significant gap from the crowds to ensure security) by the heads of state that the magazine routinely satirised. They

SOME ISSUES:

How important is freedom of speech?

Are there any situations when you think freedom of speech should not apply?

Do you think the cartoonists had the right to do what they did?

How do you think the cartoons might have affected the Muslim community in France?

The Manchester Demonstration

La liberté d'expression – un droit fondamental en France depuis 1789.

Freedom of expression – a fundamental right in France since 1789.

#JeSuisCharlie

Learn French!

included, for example, the Prime Minister of Turkey, a country which imprisons more journalists than anywhere else in the world. In fact, nine of the countries represented were in the bottom third of the World Press Freedom Index - countries where the freedom of expression that led to these murders would have been unthinkable.

The emotion that the crowd felt as they held up their pens and their signs and lit their candles was undoubtedly sincere. But was it based on reality?

There is no doubt that the editors and cartoonists at Charlie Hebdo knew the risks they took when they included Islam and the prophet Muhammad in their targets. Where other media outlets censored themselves,

Charlie Hebdo refused to treat Islam any differently from the other religions that they relentlessly mocked, such as the Catholic church. In publishing their cartoons the team at Charlie Hebdo knew that they were probably stepping beyond their normal level of provocation into an area that was inflammatory.

Charlie Hebdo was intended as an alternative view, a very left-wing, anti-establishment and anti-racist voice. Its purpose was to oppose all conservative, right-wing causes and organisations. It targeted French nationalists and all religions particularly Catholicism.

The manner in which it did this was to be deliberately offensive. In a previous magazine, members of the team had prided themselves that their output was (to quote a reader) "stupid and nasty" ("bête et méchant"), and Charlie Hebdo could certainly be that - in the long standing tradition of harsh and cruel cartoons. Its depictions of Jewish politicians, for example, can resemble some of the worst Nazi propaganda.

While on the one hand it could score an excellent point about the difference between Islam and terrorism by depicting the prophet about to be beheaded by a fundamentalist, on the other it constantly caricatured Muhammad in a way that was little different from the depictions used by the nationalists to foster hatred.

Nothing excuses the murderous attacks on the magazine and on a Jewish supermarket in Paris which followed, but it is worth understanding the atmosphere in France in which they took place. This might begin to explain, to some extent, why some Muslims in France, the UK and elsewhere said they understood the actions of the killers.

France has a large Muslim population, many of whom can trace their origins to French colonies in North Africa. While many Muslims are well integrated and see themselves as fundamentally French, there is conflict between aspects of their faith and the French constitution.

One basic principle of French public life is 'laïcité' - that religion should be kept separate from

Charlie Hebdo was intended as an alternative view... deliberately offensive.

@RLOppenheimer

Marseille Demonstration, Image © Pop H,
https://creativecommons.org/licenses/by-nd/2.0/

The Charlie Hebdo journalists were both brave and reckless

government, education and other public services. As part of this policy, obvious religious symbols are banned. Controversy arose when Muslim girls were sent home from schools for wearing their headscarves.

This was intensified by a ban on face coverings in public places. This was presented as protecting and empowering women but it was seen as an attack on freedom of choice and religious freedom. It actually restricted the freedom of those women whose cultural belief in the burqa meant that they would not leave the house without it. Some Muslims felt that the power of the state was being turned against them.

The liberal values of the French state - free speech, freedom of religion and freedom from religion - were then used by the extreme right to harass Muslims and to stir up hatred and fear.

The rich and influential are the legitimate targets of satirists who see themselves as chipping away at the power base. As part of its policy of being equally offensive to all, Charlie Hebdo was arousing the anger of Muslims in France and around the world. Few had seen the cartoons, most were neither rich nor powerful nor educated, but they were deeply insulted.

And a few were prepared and equipped to act to silence anyone who mocked their religion.

Nothing justifies the murders. No one can doubt that the staff at Charlie Hebdo were braver in their defiance than many other media organisations. But were the satirists - white, educated, middle-class people - justified in using their creativity and access to the media to persist in offending a group which included people who felt marginalised and excluded? Should they have modfied their mockery, not because of threats but because those wounded by it included the less privileged?

It is an important principle of free speech that people should be able to say things that others find hateful and offensive. Religion cannot be protected from all criticism or from all mockery. A basic tenet of democracy is the right to express controversial views that can cause offence.

How far does that right extend? Who judges if a cartoon is offensive yet effective or merely stupid and racist? Certainly this shouldn't be decided by a fanatic with a machine gun.

We can be sure that the murdered cartoonists would have been scathing in their portrayal of the world leaders attending the protest, the hypocrisy and crocodile tears from people who ban free speech. They would probably have ferociously ridiculed the combination of sentimentality and nationalism in the crowds singing the Marseillaise - and dared us to be offended by their mockery.

The Charlie Hebdo journalists were both brave and reckless. Their work was courageous but could also be repellent. Sometimes they were sharp and eye-opening and sometimes they were hostile and reactionary. By being offensive, they were protecting everyone's right to freedom of speech. That's how free speech works. It gives us the right to be wrong.

The 18th century French writer and satirist Voltaire wrote (to a priest): "Monsieur l'abbé, I detest what you write, but I would give my life to make it possible for you to continue to write."

And, in effect, that is what the slaughtered cartoonists did.

Sources: Various

UPDATE: On 19 July 2015, Laurent Sourisseau the editor of Charlie Hebdo was reported as saying that the magazine would no longer depict the Prophet Muhammad. He said the cartoons had done their job in defending the right to free expression and that they did not want the magazine to appear to be obsessed by Islam since other religions had the same faults.

Sourisseau was at the meeting when the gunmen burst in but survived by playing dead.

Work

FROM DOG FOOD TASTER TO EEL ECOLOGIST: SIX JOBS THAT ARE SURPRISINGLY ENJOYABLE

Six people talk about their unusual work, and the job satisfaction that comes with it

The first Monday of January is probably prime-time for feeling glum about work: it's ages until the next holiday, it's dark in the morning and when you get home, and it's still quite a long time until pay day. And if you're stuck in a job you don't like it could be enough to have you reaching for your CV.

But before you start hunting through the job ads, try to put things in perspective. So what else could you be doing instead? We asked six people doing some unusual jobs how much they are paid, what the worst parts are and why they enjoy their work.

Donna Ferguson

SOME ISSUES:

Which job do you think is the strangest?

And which is the most appealing?

Can you imagine doing any of these jobs?

Do you think salary or job satisfaction is most important?

What would you like to do when you are older?

SHOPPING CHANNEL PRESENTER

The job: Selling and demonstrating a wide range of products on live TV.

What it involves: Presenting hours and hours of content, while simultaneously demonstrating the products and being enthusiastic and knowledgeable about everything that you're selling. "I prepare and research as much technical and practical information as possible on every single product beforehand," says Shaun Ryan, presenter for Ideal World TV. "But you also need the ability to relate to every genre of products and to every viewer."

Typical salary: A trainee presenter would start on a minimum of £30,000, while an experienced presenter can expect over £55,000.

Worst part of the job: "The unsociable hours," says Ryan. "An experienced presenter like myself generally gets to work primetime hours which means all weekends, bank holidays and very late evenings, plus the occasional 5am shift." His worst task ever, he says, was singlehandedly having to sell some female slimming pants with a breathable gusset: "It was a very tricky hour and not my finest."

Job satisfaction: "I love the rush of live presenting and having to think on my feet every second," says Ryan. "I also get an adrenaline rush of knowing that, at times, I have thousands of viewers ordering the product that I have just been presenting."

DOG FOOD TASTER

The job: Tasting dog food to make sure it meets a premium brand's exacting quality standards.

What it involves: Opening sample tins of each freshly made batch of dog (or cat) food, smelling it and eating it. "Although dogs' palates are different to ours, taste is an important quality check to ensure each different ingredient is perfectly balanced in just the right way," says Philip Wells, the chief taster for Lily's Kitchen pet food. "Trying the food is also a good way to pick up on the nuances of the cooking; this works especially well on the dry kibbles."

Typical salary: £20,000 for an entry level job in the quality department. However, Wells says £50,000 or more is "easily achievable" for an experienced technical director who, as well tasting products, is also likely to be responsible for developing new recipes and advising the business on technical and regulatory matters.

Worst part of the job: The deadlines, for Wells, who admits he quite likes the food. The meat used in pet food has to be derived from animals passed as fit for human consumption, under the Animal Feed Regulations 2010, and he says the firm uses "human-grade freshly prepared raw food" in its recipes. He adds:"There are some pretty gruesome pet foods out there and although I don't taste them, the smell is enough to turn the stomach when I do a bit of market research."

Job satisfaction: "No two days are ever the same." It's rewarding, Wells says, that a project he has worked on will "help pets to become happier and healthier". However, he acknowledges that some of the credit must go to another "key member" of the tasting team: Lily, the border terrier.

HYGIENE TECHNICIAN

The job: Disinfecting areas that have potentially been exposed to bio-hazardous situations.

What it involves: Cleaning up crime scenes, road accidents and suicides. Clearing hoarders' houses full of rubbish, rats and excrement ... among other things. "The job is about keeping people safe," says Richard Lewis, a hygiene technician for Rentokil Specialist Hygiene. "We deal with some very disturbingly dirty sites."

Typical salary: The entry level salary is usually around £14,500 and a top salary can be up to £22,000.

Worst part of the job: Cleaning up after suicides. "You get used to the job being disgusting but the emotional side of it is still hard." You learn not to take your work home with you, he says. "You also need to have a sense of humour, as some days can be tough."

Job satisfaction: Lewis finds the variety of tasks exciting. "One day I'm cleaning up after a dead body, another day I'm in a prison cell, or 100 feet in the air being lowered down into a silo to clean it." He also takes pride in the transformation he brings about: "It's satisfying to return a potentially hazardous site back to a safe environment. And it benefits society."

EXPEDITION LEADER FOR A GROUP OF TEENAGERS

The job: Leading groups of 15- to 18-year-olds through testing experiences overseas that demand high levels of physical fitness.

What it involves: Motivating and looking after inexperienced teenagers in tough, unfamiliar environments, far away from their usual creature comforts. "For many young people it is the first time they have had to face the responsibility and consequences of their actions," says Vanessa Johnson, a World Challenge Expedition leader, who takes groups trekking over Kilimanjaro. "My job is to try to make sure it happens in an unseen envelope of reasonable safety."

Typical salary: Depending on experience, you can earn £1,200 to £2,500 for a four-week-long expedition. Each teenager pays £4,900 – so expectations are high.

Worst part of the job: Sorting out injuries and illnesses. "I had two Australians once who climbed on a rooftop for a lark – forgetting that, if they had fallen, we were two days away from medical assistance and all the comforts of a developed hospital," says Johnson. Her charges also often express surprise at the cold showers and humble toilet facilities.

Job satisfaction: "I like seeing individuals return home with a reformed attitude to their life and an improved understanding of the worthlessness of many 'essential' material possessions," says Johnson.

EEL ECOLOGIST

The job: Conserving the critically endangered European eel.

What it involves: To monitor the size of the endangered eels ecologists wade into the Thames and other London rivers and marshes full of eels, sometimes up to their armpits, and reach into a net filled with up to 20 adult eels to grab one with their bare hands. "Adult eels can be a metre long or even larger, and weigh up to 2kg. They're not at all dangerous but they are almost pure muscle and they can be a little bit slimy," says Stephen Mowat, an eel conservationist and ecologist for the Zoological Society of London. "We have to weigh and measure them, and they wriggle, a lot. It's difficult to look professional while crawling on the ground chasing an eel across the grass."

Worst part of the job: "Eels are really tricky creatures to work with – and getting outsmarted by an eel can be quite embarrassing," says Mowat. "You also have to be ready to jump from one project to the next. I once had to dissect a tub of dead eel guts (and stomach the smell) to examine parasites living in their swim bladders, moments before jumping into a suit for a meeting with government officials. I remembered to wash my hands." But for Mowat the worst part of the job is definitely not handling the eels – he believes baby eels (known as elvers) are "as cute as pandas": "The worst thing about the job is regularly learning how much damage we, the British population, are doing to the environment."

Job satisfaction: "Getting to work outdoors and seeing British wildlife up close is the best part of the job," says Mowat. "Eels are beautiful creatures and working with eels doesn't just benefit the eel, it helps whole river systems, estuaries and coastal habitats. That is something worth working on."

Image: © ZSL

BIOGAS ENGINEER

The job: Setting up biogas plants in developing countries.

What the job involves: Linking a system of digesters – which can be filled with human excrement, animal dung and other waste products – to toilets to produce a biogas that can be used for cooking and lighting. "You have to know what size and shape the mixing pit needs to be, how to create the optimum temperature for digestion and where to situate the biogas plant," says Baburam Paudel, chief technical officer in Nepal for the charity Renewable World. "You also have convince poor communities that poo can be productive – many are repelled by the idea of connecting their toilets to their kitchens."

Typical salary: An entry level salary is around £10,000 while a typical salary for a chief technical officer is £30,000.

Worst part of the job: For Paudel, it's seeing people struggling to survive on very little income. But, he admits, anyone who won't change a nappy would struggle. "You have to be willing to get your hands dirty during the build process and inspections. Unsurprisingly, the anaerobic digestion (the process that takes place when bacteria eat the decomposing waste and produce methane) smells like rotten eggs. It can be disgusting and there is no room for mistakes."

Job satisfaction: "I find it immensely satisfying to know that I am helping people to increase their incomes and allowing girls to attend school by replacing the need to collect firewood," says Paudel. "My work improves the health and hygiene of whole communities."

The Guardian, 5 January 2015
© Guardian News & Media 2015

Make job sharing more rewarding

Anne Johnson

SOME ISSUES:

What benefits would there be if more people jobshared?

How might it affect people, the family, health, private and social life?

How might it affect society as a whole?

Why do you think more companies don't actively seek jobshare staff?

Do you think more companies should be encouraged to split up roles into jobshares?

A brief missive from inside The Flexibility Trap. That's the title of a report from the Timewise Foundation, a social enterprise that supports and lobbies for those who want flexibility in their careers, without writing off their promotion prospects.

It makes depressing reading because, though more than a quarter of Britain's labour force work part-time or flexibly, this research shows that most (77%) feel trapped in their present jobs because quality part-time vacancies are as rare as hen's teeth. Three-quarters of the 1,000 part-timers consulted said they haven't had a single promotion since switching to fewer hours. Around 40% had taken jobs well below their skill and (full time equivalent) pay level. And many have been obliged to accept demotion (known in the recruitment business as "backsliding").

Of course, this issue isn't just about fairness and wasted talent. It's also about gender, since most part-time workers are women, usually trying to fit paid work around caring responsibilities. Currently an estimated 600,000 British mothers (including rising numbers of single mothers obliged to look for work by benefit changes) say they feel "locked out" of the workforce. In some cases that's because previously full-time workers are accepting part-time jobs because that's all they can get.

It's easy to see how this combination of backsliding,

My jobsharer and I represented excellent value for money. Together we were more productive and energetic than one stressed-out worker

being trapped in part-time work and being locked out of it altogether is contributing to a widening gender pay gap. Only 3% of part-time jobs advertised pay more than the full time equivalent of £20,000 a year.

That's why Karen Mattison and Emma Stewart got together to form the Timewise Foundation, which has launched an online careers service (womenlikeus.org.uk) with funding from the Cabinet Office.

I should declare an interest in this subject, as I've worked four days a week for several years, following a period of jobsharing, while my children were small. These days people often say things like: "You'd be running that place by now if you'd always worked full time." Maybe, maybe not. I certainly kissed goodbye to any serious promotion prospects by becoming a part-timer.

Why? Because, while some employers

(academia, retail banking and the public sector, for instance) are better than others, Britain more than anywhere retains a rigid work culture in which there is a false correlation between commitment and long hours. Conversely, jobsharers and part-timers are still perceived as not doing a "proper job". It still carries a stigma. Just imagine the curl on Alan Sugar's lip if

Why shouldn't flexibility be the default option? Why shouldn't most job ads carry a rider to the effect that part-time or flexible working will be considered?

a candidate for The Apprentice requested a four-day week.

Yet, looking back, I'm convinced that my jobsharer and I represented excellent value for money. Together we were more productive and energetic than one stressed-out worker trying to juggle full-time work and childcare could ever have been. Perhaps, grateful to have a decent work-life balance, I curbed my own expectations. Now, as I contemplate my dotage on a dot-sized pension, I hope my daughters don't have to make such a costly sacrifice.

Maybe the Coalition's Children and Families Act, extending the right to request flexible working to all workers, will help dismantle society's perception of traditional gender stereotyping in the workplace, even if the 26-week qualifying period will continue to act as a barrier to women getting jobs.

Ultimately, wouldn't life in Britain be improved by challenging the polarisation between work-rich time-poor dual income households where parents regularly fall asleep trying to read bedtime stories to their children and families struggling to survive on a patchwork of dead-end part-time jobs? Why shouldn't flexibility be the default option? Why shouldn't most job ads carry a rider to the effect that part-time or flexible working will be considered?

Meanwhile, we need more inspirational examples of those like four-day a week Katie Bickerstaffe, chief executive of Dixons UK and Ireland and Belinda Earl, three-day a week style director at M&S, who feature in the Timewise Power Part-Time Top 50 and who challenge those who still insist that such a combination is an oxymoron.

Herald Scotland, 10 July 2013
Reproduced with permission of
Herald & Times Group

GHOST JOBS, HALF LIVES: how agency workers 'get by' in Britain's shadow economy

Aditya Chakrabortty

SOME ISSUES:

What do you think are the pros and cons of casual work?

Why do you think companies might prefer to employ casual workers?

Should companies have to provide security and benefits for employees on lower, casual hours?

What should be done to make work more secure for people on lower hours?

Before he urged bosses last week to dish out pay rises, David Cameron should have met Martin. If nothing else, the encounter might have given him pause before that "Come on, chaps" routine. Because Martin could have told him of an entire world of work that the public hardly ever hears about - whose misery runs as deep as any life on those much-publicised zero-hours contracts. His story confirms a truth some frontbench politicians admit in private but none dare acknowledge in public: that something in the jobs market is fundamentally broken.

Martin isn't his real name and, to prevent any reprisals, I shall obscure a few key details. In a curious way that fits his story. Martin, you see, is an unperson, in a workforce that is breeding unpeople by the hundreds of thousands.

He works at the Jacob's biscuit factory in Liverpool, although he's not employed by the firm. Instead, he works for Prime Time Recruitment, one of Britain's biggest suppliers of contract labour. He does the same work as Jacob's own staff, and often substitutes for their absences - but is on the minimum wage; they get paid over £2 an hour more. They're on a rota, while he has to wait by his phone for each shift. His holiday and sick-pay entitlements are much worse, too. Jacob's staff enjoy access to a workplace gym and medical centre; when Martin had an accident with a forklift truck, the medical centre turned him away, telling him to find his own doctor.

Martin never knows when he will be working: just last week, he was rung up in the morning to be told he had 45 minutes to his next shift. Nor does he know where he will be working: his agency regularly offers him work in a factory in Blackpool. As Prime Time pointed out to me on Monday, that's within a contractual 25-mile radius as the crow flies. But as Martin demonstrates on Google Maps, it's over 50 miles by road, and the travel costs mean that a six-hour shift would only earn him just over £3 an hour. When he turns down such impossible jobs, the agency then uses a legal loophole to chalk him up as unavailable for work and pays him nothing.

Martin's phone, with its texts and calls from Prime Time, has more control over his life than he does. As a middle-aged father, he's borrowed to cover food and fuel bills, and "I've not known when I'll be able to pay anything back". Holidays? Forget it. He points at one of two toddlers messing around on the living-room floor: her first Christmas was "nearly ruined" for lack of money.

What makes this different from zero-hours work is Martin isn't directly employed by his workplace. But the effect is almost the same: the workers and their families are burdened with all the insecurity and powerlessness, while their employers enjoy the flexibility of labour on tap.

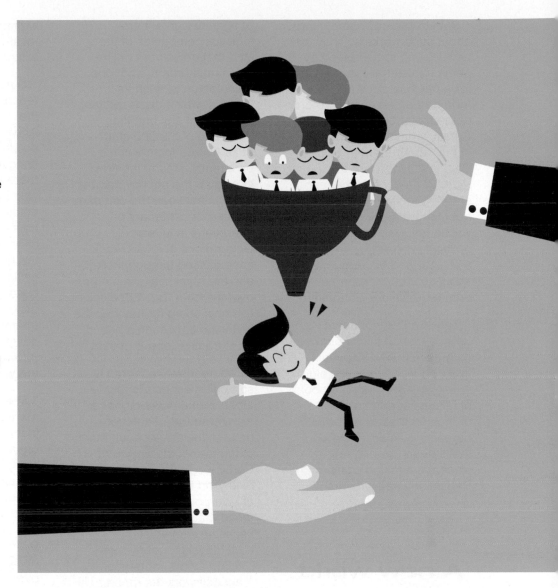

The workers and their families are burdened with all the insecurity and powerlessness, while their employers enjoy the flexibility of labour on tap.

Add the estimated 1.2 million agency workers to the 600,000 on zero-hours contracts, and you have a shadow workforce of about 1.8 million unpeople, enjoying none of the security that should come with employment in a rich country. Thanks to official neglect, so much about these unpeople is unknown. We don't even know how many employment agencies there are, let alone how many names they have on their books.

But we can say some things about such workers. They are never going to be helped by prime ministerial exhortations for a pay rise. As such, they form part of the answer to one of the major conundrums in Britain: what's gone wrong in our labour market. This Wednesday will see the monthly ritual of a jobs report showing record employment, but meagre wage rises. This will be followed by Labour politicians attacking Tory austerity, and government spokespeople assuring us that brighter days are just ahead.

The shadow workforce tells us that all this is bunk. Its growth points the way to a new world in which big employers draw upon a pool of casual labour, stripped of most of their rights and bargaining power. It's a pool that's been growing fast since the banking crisis. Particularly heavy users

of agency workers are logistics companies of the kind that deliver our online Christmas orders, and food manufacturers such as Jacob's, which disclosed last year that at any one time up to 250 of the 900 staff at its Aintree factory could be agency. (Today the firm estimated the agency number at 70.) Last year, the company marked its centenary of operations in Liverpool. Generations of locals would have passed through there, and the royal seal still hangs over the door. But those social ties now count for nothing; the factory is becoming a hub in an extractive labour market.

The shadow workforce is spreading especially fast in those economies that never recovered from Thatcher's great industrial wipeout. Much of the former steel town of Corby is now just agency land. And in Martin's home of Liverpool, the city council found that of the 13,771 vacancies advertised in Merseyside, nearly half - 6,600 - were for temporary agency work. Its report, published last autumn, in effect punctures all the smug forecasts that the jobs market will soon turn a corner. What it tells you is that for people like Martin, in hollowed-out economies like his suburb of Liverpool, the market isn't suddenly going to right itself. And until that happens - as Barry Kushner, a Labour councillor, points out - the housing association will continue to rack up arrears, and the

waiting list for advice at the local Citizens Advice bureau will grow.

Sure, there are supply teachers enjoying the freedom that agency status brings. And one imagines that others do skip from temp job to fully fledged career. But elsewhere there are people like Martin, who have no choice. He's holding out for a permanent staff position, yet can't think of anyone who has made the leap. Nor can he sign on while looking for other work, because that would count as making himself voluntarily unemployed and lead to being deprived of Jobseeker's Allowance. So he is stuck at the very bottom of the pile.

There are winners from Martin's position, of course - just not him and his family, or us taxpayers. The workfare company A4e, which sent Martin to the factory, gets a fee from the taxpayer for placing a warm body in a job. Jacob's, an arm of a £2bn business, gets cheap labour with none of the pesky overheads or obligations. Middleman Prime Time, part of a group with a £500m annual turnover, takes its cut and was until last August getting government funding on top. The losers are Martin who, for all his wit and diligence, faces years on the minimum wage; and us, who top up his poverty pay with benefits.

A few hours after Martin and I say goodbye, he texts me with a message for you, the readers. What you need to know about agency workers, he says, is, "they don't live, they get by".

The Guardian, 19 January 2015
© Guardian News & Media 2015

A new world in which big employers draw upon a pool of casual labour, stripped of most of their rights and bargaining power

Complete
Issues

understanding our world

Published by Carel Press Ltd
4 Hewson St, Carlisle CA2 5AU
Tel +44 (0)1228 538928,
Fax 591816
office@carelpress.co.uk
www.carelpress.co.uk
This collection © 2016
Christine A Shepherd & Chas White

Acknowledgements
Designer: Anne Louise Kershaw
Editorial team: Anne Louise
Kershaw, Debbie Maxwell, Christine
A Shepherd, Chas White
Subscriptions: Ann Batey (Manager),
Brenda Hughes

We wish to thank all those writers,
editors, photographers, press
agencies and wire services who
have given permission to reproduce
copyright material. Every effort
has been made to trace copyright
holders of material but in a few
cases this has not been possible.
The publishers would be glad to
hear from anyone who has not been
consulted.

Cover design:
Anne Louise Kershaw
Front cover photo: © Bryan Sutter /
Demotix/Demotix/Press Association
Images

**British Library
Cataloguing in Publication Data**

Essential Articles 2016: The articles
you need on the issues that matter.
1. Social problems – Study and
teaching (Secondary) – Great Britain
2. Social sciences – Study and
teaching (Secondary) – Great Britain
   I. Shepherd, Christine A
II. White, C
   361.00712 41
   ISBN 978-1-905600-48-9

Printed by Finemark, Poland